Dr Robyn Wrigley-Carr is Senior Lecturer in theology and spirituality at Alphacrucis College, S ·
the University of St Andrews, exa
as a spiritual director.

As well as being an academic,
retreat leader.

She is the editor of *Evelyn Unde*
Board and Book Reviews Editor
Spirituality and a co-opted member of the Executive Committee
of the British Association for the Study of Spirituality (2019–2020).

Baron Friedrich von Hügel (1852–1925)

THE SPIRITUAL FORMATION
OF EVELYN UNDERHILL

Robyn Wrigley-Carr

First published in Great Britain in 2020

Society for Promoting Christian Knowledge
36 Causton Street
London SW1P 4ST
www.spck.org.uk

Scripture quotations are taken from the ESV Bible (The Holy Bible, English
Standard Version), copyright © 2001 by Crossway, a publishing ministry
of Good News Publishers. Used by permission. All rights reserved.

British Library Cataloguing-in-Publication Data
A catalogue record for this book is available from the British Library

ISBN 978–0–281–08157–8
eBook ISBN 978–0–281–08158–5

Typeset by Falcon Oast Graphic Art Ltd

First printed in Great Britain by Ashford Colour Press
Subsequently digitally reprinted in Great Britain

eBook by Falcon Oast Graphic Art Ltd

Produced on paper from sustainable forests

To Gavin, Hannah, Laura and Emma, with much love

Evelyn Underhill (1875–1941)
Courtesy of the House of Retreat, Pleshey

Contents

Foreword by Eugene Peterson   ix

1 Introducing the Baron   1
2 Introducing Evelyn Underhill   18
3 The Baron's spiritual formation of Evelyn Underhill   48
4 Motherhood of souls: Evelyn the spiritual director   85
5 Motherhood of souls: Evelyn the retreat leader   113

Afterword   138
Notes   141
References   166

CONTENTS

Foreword

I grew up around people who identified the Christian life with in-flated emotional states. Grandiosity was epidemic. The ordinary was for people 'without Christ'. We were in training for ecstasy. I soon tired of it. I began looking for men and women who had somehow managed to grow up. Locating them wasn't always easy or imme-diate. But patience paid off. I have never been in a congregation in which I have not found them. Some became friends and guides. For others it was enough to know and observe them from a distance.

I soon learned that the way to Christian maturity is through the commonplace. I had to unlearn much – learn not to overreach, not to strain for high-flown epithets or resolutions, to stay as true as I could to the grain of life as I found it in the lives around me in the congregation and Scriptures which formed my identity.

The most formative of these guides for me, though, is a man I never met. Baron Friedrich von Hügel died seven years before I was born. As measured by an annual physical exam and my academic degrees I was certified as an adult, but measured by Paul's standard of maturity I was still a child 'tossed to and fro . . . by every wind of doctrine' (Ephesians 4.14; esv) – far from being mature vocationally or spiritually. One of my guides, the Quaker philosopher Douglas Steere, recommended that I read von Hügel's books. I hadn't read many pages before realizing that I was in the presence of a mature Christian who knew what it meant to measure up to the full stature of Christ (Ephesians 4.13).

A layperson, von Hügel was a spiritual director of great wisdom in the early decades of the twentieth century. He lived on a pri-vate income and gave a lifetime of attention to the life of the Spirit and to the lives of his contemporaries. There is a kind of German ponderousness in the way he writes, but I find him to be the most sane, balanced and wise mind/spirit of my acquaintance. By sinking himself into the deeply lived truth of the centuries, he provided a mature centre for many others in his counsel and writings. He was absolutely impervious to the fads and fashions of both culture and Church that swirled around him like flies. Most of his spiritual direction was in handwritten personal letters in any of several languages. So, as we read them, we are always in touch with the actual stuff of life being lived out in an actual named person. No great generalizations. No pompous 'wisdom' from on high. As I read von Hügel, I am constantly aware that I am in the presence of a man who is primarily interested in *living* the Christian faith and living it well, not merely talking about it, not just arguing over it.

Von Hügel supplied me with metaphors and an image that provided a shaping influence on my life. I've been reading him ever since. I hope that you will too. The Baron cannot be summarized. The intricate complexities that result in his lurid clarities can only, I am convinced, be received at first hand from his own writing.

When I encountered von Hügel, I was no stranger to the Christian faith. But Church as an institution in time and place, theology as critical thinking about God, and prayer as the practice of resurrection were like separate planets in orbit around the wobbly centre that was me. Von Hügel used the analogy of physical growth – infancy, adolescence, adulthood – to elaborate on the integration of the Christian life: infancy corresponds to the institutional; adolescence corresponds to the intellectual; and adulthood is analogous to prayer as everything we live through coheres in a resurrection life. The three stages are ages through which we develop into maturity. No stage can be omitted. And no stage can be left behind. Maturity develops as each is assimilated into the next, resulting in a single coherent life.

Much of von Hügel's deeply lived and extensively pondered experience as a Christian layperson, rooted and grounded in the life of Christ and at the same time in the earthly and domestic realities of a wife, three daughters and a dog named Puck, comes to us via letters written in his own hand to an astonishing number of correspondents. A constant note in his counsel, consistently sounded, is that the road to a life of maturity is not a 'yellow brick road', but involves considerable difficulties that cannot be bulldozed away. This portion of a letter to his niece is thematic:

> When at eighteen, I made up my mind to go into moral and religious training, the great soul and mind who took me in hand – a noble Dominican – warned me – 'You want to grow in virtue, to serve God, to love Christ? Well, you will grow in and attain these things if you will make them a slow and sure, an utterly real, mountain step-plod and ascent, willing to have to camp for weeks or months in spiritual desolation, darkness and emptiness at different stages in your march and growth. All demand for constant light . . . all attempt at eliminating or minimizing the cross, and trial, is so much soft folly and puerile trifling.'[1]

Magnificent as the Christian life is, when it comes to growing up in Christ, von Hügel will permit no shortcuts, no romanticizing that depreciates the ordinary, 'no cutting of knots however difficult, no revolt against, no evasion of abuses however irritating or benumbing',[2] but an insistence that the road to maturity necessarily follows a route that, in his words, often is 'obtuse-seeming, costingly wise, not brilliantly clever, ruminant, slow, if you will, stupid, ignored, defeated, yet life-creating'.[3]

It is a well-documented axiom in Christian living that we can know this life only by *becoming* it, growing in every way into a maturity that is sane, stable and robust. The Apostle Paul in Ephesians, with the Baron seconding the motion, would have us settle for nothing less than the 'full stature of Christ'.

*

In our increasingly secularized culture there is also, surprisingly enough, a widespread interest in what is often termed 'spirituality'. This interest is often accompanied by the disclaimer 'I love Jesus but I hate the Church'. The 'Church' is often what is designated 'institutional religion'. This widespread interest in 'spirituality' is in many ways a result of disillusionment and frustration with institutional religion. As a result, the new spirituality avoids all the trappings of liturgy and finance, fundraising campaigns and buildings, ecclesiastical bureaucracies, hair-splitting decisions on theology, legislating and domesticating the Spirit. This new spirituality sets itself in opposition to all that. It encourages us to explore our higher consciousness, cultivate beauty and awareness, find friends of like mind with whom we can converse and pray and travel. Spirituality is an inward journey to the depths of our souls. Spirituality is dismissive of doctrines and building campaigns, formal worship and theologians.

There is something to be said for this, but not much. It is true that the world of religion is responsible for an enormous amount of cruelty and oppression, war and prejudice and hate, pomp and circumstance. Being religious does not translate into being good or trustworthy across the board. Religion is one of the best covers for sin of almost all kinds. Pride, anger, lust and greed are vermin that flourish under the floorboards of religion. Those of us who are identified with institutions or vocations in religion can't be too vigilant. The devil does some of his best work behind stained glass.

So it is interesting to observe that Jesus, who in abridged form is quite popular with the non-church crowd, was not anti-institutional. Jesus said 'Follow me', and then regularly led his followers into the two primary religious institutional structures of his day: the synagogue and the Temple. Neither institution was without its inadequacies, faults and failures. The Temple, especially, was shot through with corruption, venality, injustice and discrimination. Caiaphas and his henchmen had installed vendors in the Temple courts, controlled taxation, made huge profits on the sacrificial animals and presided over the daily prayers and the great festivals. The synagogues had become well known for excluding outsiders (women, tax collectors, the blind and maimed).

Those who followed Jesus followed him into those buildings, religious *institutions*. After his ascension, they continued to frequent both Temple (until its destruction in AD 70) and synagogue. I don't think we are going to find much support in Jesus for the contemporary preference for the golf course as a place of worship over the First Baptist Church. Given the stories that the four Gospels offer us, it doesn't seem likely that, if Jesus showed up today and we were invited to follow him, we would find ourselves taking a Sunday morning stroll out of the city, away from asphalted parking lots, away from church buildings filled with people more interested in gossip than in the gospel, away from the city noise and smells to a quiet meadow and a quiet stream for a morning of meditation among the wild flowers.

We sometimes say, thoughtlessly I think, that the Church is people, not a building. I'm not so sure. Synagogues and temples, cathedrals, chapels and storefront meeting halls, provide continuity in a set-apart place and worshipping community for Jesus to work his will among his people. A place, a designated building, collects stories and develops associations that give local depth, breadth and continuity to our experience of following Jesus. We must not try to be more spiritual than Jesus in this business. Following Jesus means following him into sacred buildings that have a lot of sinners in them, some of them very conspicuous sinners. Jesus doesn't seem to mind.

A spirituality that has no institutional structure or support very soon becomes self-indulgent, subjective and one-generational. A wise and learned student of these things, Baron Friedrich von Hügel, the subject of this brilliantly written book, thought long and hard about this and insisted that institutional religion is absolutely necessary, being an aspect of the incarnational core that is characteristic of the Christian faith.

Von Hügel provides us with a brilliant image for understanding what we are dealing with here. The Christian life, he wrote, is a tree: it begins underground in an invisible root system embedded in dirt and millions of micro-organisms. Nobody ever sees that depth-dimension of the tree's life, but nor does anyone doubt that it is there. The evidence of its life is visible in its leaves, which are immersed in the invisibilities of air, receiving life from above. What connects the roots in the soil that we can't see to the air above, which we can't see, is a thin, delicate membrane that girdles the trunk of the tree but is also invisible beneath the bark. The membrane has a name, cambium, and the flow of life from roots to leaves goes through it. But until the tree is cut down we never see the cambium. It is hidden under the very visible but thoroughly dead bark. The rough, dead bark protects the hidden, delicate, living cambium. The actual *life* of the tree (roots, cambium, air) is invisible.

Religious institutions are to the spiritual life what bark is to the cambium. Most of what we see when we look at a forest of white oak trees, particularly in the winter when their leaves have fallen, is dead. But the dead bark protects the inner life of the tree. The more intimate and personal an activity is – having sex or eating a meal, for instance – the more likely we are to develop rituals and conventions to protect them from profanation, disease or destruction. The most intimate and intensely personal of all human activities is the life of the spirit – our worship, prayer and meditation, believing and obeying. But, without the protection of ritual, doctrine and authority, which it is easy (and common) to consider lifeless and dead, Christian spirituality is vulnerable to reduction and desecration. It is also essential to note that, while the bark both hides and protects the cambium, it does not create it – the life comes from invisibilities below and above, soil and air – all the operations of the Trinity.

When Jesus says 'Follow me', and we follow, people will continue to see us entering our churches and working for our mission organizations. But most of who we are becoming as we follow Jesus – our Spirit-formed life – they won't see. They won't see the massive invisibilities into which we are sinking our roots, or the endless atmosphere above us, from which we receive the light of life, our lives reaching, reaching, reaching to the depths, reaching across the horizon and reaching to the heights.

For over fifty years now Baron Friedrich von Hügel has been, for me and my friends, among the wisest of masters in guiding us into a persevering, lifelong obedience in following Jesus. He often said, 'stampedes and panics are of NO earthly use'.[4] Undisciplined energy is useless or worse than useless. When the tactics of fear are used in Christian communities to motivate a life of trust in God and love of neighbour, habits of maturity never have a chance to develop. And when consumer satisfactions of happiness and success are on offer it is even worse. When the Christian community reduces its preaching, teaching and witnessing to punchy slogans and clichés, it abandons the richly nuanced intricacies that bring all the parts of our lives into a supple and grace-filled wholeness. All who let themselves be seduced into taking promised shortcuts of instant gratification that bypass the way of the cross eventually find that the so-called gratifications turn into addictions, incapacitating them for mature relationships in household, workplace and congregation.

The book that you hold in your hand, written by Dr Robyn Wrigley-Carr, spiritual director and professor, provides us with the most extensive and inviting introduction to this by now classic contribution to the art of spiritual direction, available now to a generation that 'knew not Joseph' (Exodus 1.8).

Eugene H. Peterson (1932–2018)
Professor Emeritus of Spiritual Theology
Regent College, Vancouver

1

Introducing the Baron
(1852–1925)

'To sanctify is the biggest thing out.' These words of his ring in
my mind. They express what he was, what he meant, what he
wished most to do. His whole life lies in them. He tried to . . .
sanctify our lives. He loved, and he wanted to teach us to love.[1]
(Gwendolen Greene)

One likes to help people.[2]
(von Hügel)

It was Eugene Peterson who introduced me to Baron Friedrich
von Hügel. I had asked Eugene for the names of three people who
had greatly influenced him, in terms of spiritual formation, and had
written letters of spiritual nurture. Friedrich von Hügel was the
first name Eugene provided, and thus began a journey of coming
to know 'the Baron' (as he was affectionately called), a man of great
substance, stature and spiritual influence. I was immediately struck
by the Baron's largeness of soul, passion for God, spiritual depth,
kindness, humility and creative thought. Von Hügel had a striking
openness to new ideas, yet possessed a strong, established centre
that anchored him, allowing him to explore the unknown from a
place of centred stability. He had an immense intellect but, more
significantly, an enlarged heart and a gift of spiritual discernment
that could 'read' people and wisely nurture them. After immersing
myself in von Hügel's life and writings, I later discovered Evelyn
Underhill. Reading Evelyn's work, I couldn't help but hear echoes of

1

the Baron. I regard von Hügel as the living soulguide who had the most significant impact on her. Evelyn herself declared, 'I owe him my whole spiritual life.'[3]

This book explores both the spiritual formation that Evelyn Underhill received from von Hügel and her subsequent spiritual formation of others, through spiritual direction and retreats. But to understand von Hügel's spiritual nurture of Evelyn it's first necessary to briefly consider some aspects of the Baron's personal narrative and context.

The Baron's story

Baron Friedrich von Hügel was a Catholic layperson and religious philosopher who embodied an exceptional ability to explore and guide people into the deep things of God. While he was celebrated in his day as a 'religious genius',[4] our 'greatest theologian'[5] and the 'most learned man living',[6] I consider his most enduring contribution to have been as a guide and encourager of souls. I would argue that his spiritual direction was the central axis that framed his intellectual contribution.[7] The Baron's spiritual nurture profoundly shaped many famous individuals, including two remarkable writers in Christian spirituality – Evelyn Underhill and Eugene Peterson. Both these recipients of von Hügel's soul care have reached much broader audiences than the Baron directly influenced himself.

A vivid image of von Hügel is of a tall, thin man, walking the streets of Kensington in London in his massive cloak, top hat, black woollen gloves and cream umbrella, leaning over while shouting, as a deaf man does, the 'most intimate spiritual advice'.[8]

The Baron's life story has been effectively portrayed in Michael de la Bédoyère's biography. The reliability of this portrait was affirmed by von Hügel's daughter, Thekla, who indicated that, where many had 'misunderstood' her father, de la Bédoyère portrayed the 'true character & aim' of her father's life and soul.[9] So what are some of the highlights of von Hügel's life story that are relevant to his spiritual nurture of Evelyn Underhill?

A cosmopolitan, ecumenical flavour

The people, environments and ideas dominating von Hügel's childhood provide some insight into his highly original and complex persona. He was born in Florence, the eldest son of a Rhineland baron in the Austro-Hungarian diplomatic service. He never really knew his father who was fifty-seven years old when he was born, when his mother was aged only twenty-one. Von Hügel had a younger brother, who became the first curator of the Von Hügel Institute in Cambridge, and a younger sister, who became a nun.

The nature of their father's diplomatic vocation meant the family moved around Europe, with the children never attending school but being educated by tutors of various religious persuasions. The Baron lived his first eight years in Florence, where his mother's Anglican friend taught him the rudiments of religion from a Roman Catechism. Von Hügel was absolutely heartbroken when the tutor had to leave because the family moved to Brussels in 1860. In Brussels von Hügel was tutored by a German Catholic historian, who was also a Lutheran pastor, for seven years before Baron Carl retired and the family moved to Torquay, England. In Devon von Hügel was taught geology by a Quaker and broad-minded scientist, and in later adult life he learned Hebrew from a rabbi. So, while he always viewed himself as a Roman Catholic, von Hügel's formation included many diverse religious influences, which helped him become deeply ecumenical. As a spiritual director, his impact was arguably greater on Protestants than on Catholics, as some Catholics were suspicious of his earlier involvement in the Catholic modernist crisis.

Von Hügel's cosmopolitan upbringing gave him a sense of always being a foreigner. With friends scattered across Europe, he felt culturally dislocated and this was one of the great trials of his life. This was further exacerbated by the diversity of his family lineage, with an Austro-German father and a Scottish mother. Despite living his adult life in England, the Baron never succeeded in becoming or even looking English. When he first arrived in England, a man declared that he would not walk with von Hügel as he was not wearing the correct tie. Von Hügel always felt a subtle difference in both temper and instinct from even his closest English friends.[10]

The Baron's native tongue was German and throughout his life he maintained a strong German accent. His rich international upbringing meant that he was fluent in several languages, which enabled him to communicate with intellectuals across Europe and to read works in their original language. As a baron of the Roman Empire, he had the luxury of being a scholar with private means, supplementing his income with his publications.

Education and intellectual development

A desire to cross-fertilize insights from a variety of Christian traditions led to von Hügel setting up and coordinating the London Society for the Study of Religion (LSSR) in 1904. Members were deliberately chosen to represent a variety of denominations. Von Hügel recorded being 'profoundly helped' in his thought development and the Catholicism of his soul by the Lutheran Ernst Troeltsch and the Calvinist Norman Kemp Smith.[11]

Many attribute the originality of the Baron's thinking to the fact that he never attended a university, so his thought was not flattened out by the fixed curriculums of formal education.[12] This lack of institutionalized education, coupled with his sense of always being a foreign outsider, gave von Hügel a freedom from many of the fads in scholarship that were associated with particular locations. As someone who possessed a unique intellectual freedom, he critiqued those who had been misled and distracted by the immediate fashions of the day.[13]

A passion for science provided von Hügel with a methodology of working from the known to the unknown, examining life as it is and as it surrounds us – he even investigated leaf lice as a child, recording careful observations.[14] Von Hügel loved geology, and viewed it as a balancing corrective to religious thinking, which enabled him to develop a 'double consciousness' whereby he would carefully examine the evidence.[15] This attitude of discovery transferred to his research into the mysteries of soul and spirit. He endeavoured to live the spiritual life, penetrate the living realities and then express his discoveries.[16] A key value was his desire to *experience* any area that he discussed in writing. This lived, experiential posture, open to whatever truth there was to discover through exploration from all angles, was the Baron's approach in his studies of Scripture and mysticism. He desired a humble posture, seeking God and his reality, staying open and teachable rather than being 'narrow-minded' or '*superior*'.[17]

Ill health enabling a balanced scholarship

Delicate health led to von Hügel's scholarship being balanced by other activities. As he could manage to work at his academic studies only in the morning, he spent his afternoons taking daily walks, resting, talking with friends or spiritual directees, or visiting churches. When he was unwell, he spent days in solitude, lying still. Von Hügel's ill health forced him to reflect and pray through his studies, giving his writing time to percolate, for 'living and growing into it'.[18] He described these enforced breaks as his greatest crosses, yet hoped that his work might bear certain qualities that would otherwise be absent.[19] His daughter Hildegard believed that her father's ongoing illnesses added authenticity to his writings. She recalled how he spoke of the days of ill health enabling him to get nearer to great realities, deepening and strengthening his work through suffering. His face illumined with joy as he spoke of how suffering teaches more than any amount of learning.[20]

As a young man, von Hügel had a severe attack of typhus, which left him with a significant hearing impairment and suffering permanently from nervous ill health. His deafness was a tremendous trial, which made engaging in social intercourse difficult, hence his tendency to lecture rather than to engage with others dialogically. The Baron's hearing impairment and delicate health kept him relatively isolated. One Catholic priest recalled a talk von Hügel gave to Oxford students in 1918 in which he defended the reality of evil and the devil. A stormy discussion broke out and von Hügel revealed his sense of humour when he told the priest, 'I thank God for my deafness because during the discussion period I think they were rather critical of me, but I couldn't hear and was able to say my prayers.'[21]

Spiritual development

Von Hügel described his vivid sense as a child of God's presence, both through the natural world – nature environing him – and as a mysterious divine presence in the silence of the Florentine churches.[22] By the time he was thirteen, his religious sense was already strongly awake, his mind penetrated by a Spirit distinct from himself – his religion's 'thirst and support' drawn from '*what is*'.[23] But this was coupled with a strong sense from childhood that beauty comes from God. He believed that the religious sense in souls becomes narrow, hard, vague and empty, without an aesthetic capacity.[24]

Alongside aesthetics, von Hügel developed the conviction early on that a complete response to God requires the senses and the body, not just the mind. He recorded an episode in his boyhood, when a man spoke to him about the principles of anti-body and anti-senses. This man insisted that religion really had nothing to do with anything but the mind, with 'certain thoughts instilled' into our minds by the 'other mind', God.[25] Von Hügel found this notion of the mind without the body's energizing as 'thin, abstract, doctrinaire, inhuman', and thought it an approach that would drive him into 'endless self-preoccupation' instead of towards God.[26] He recognized this as extremely unbalanced, eclipsing the body and its senses as vehicles for the awakening of our spirit.[27]

A turning point in von Hügel's conviction that God answers prayer came from an experience as a youth outside Mainz Cathedral. He saw a woman run into the church, clutching her dead baby; as she threw herself on the altar, her sobs gradually quietened, and she left the church peaceful, with a radiant, glowing face.[28] Von Hügel recalled this image throughout his life, sharing it with spiritual directees.

Several people nurtured von Hügel during his youth. As a boy, he would visit Canon Agar, a saintly soul who spoke of the Church's worldliness and its constant need of saints – enfolding the Baron with the old Church at its best.[29] After his bout of typhus, von Hügel spent a year in Vienna, where he underwent a religious crisis and was helped by Father Raymond Hocking. Von Hügel remembered Hocking as a mystically minded Dominican, who was an unforgettable example and a silent influence, teaching that the ascetic lifestyle was lived for God to keep alive the spirit of renunciation and sacrifice.[30] During this season, von Hügel experienced the world as distant and cold, and Hocking taught him that the Christian life often consists of desolation.[31] Hocking's rich self-renunciation braced the Baron over many years.

When von Hügel returned to England, he was an outsider, as a European, in English Catholicism, so he drew inspiration from the pre-Reformation Catholic tradition. Several diverse influences further formed his spiritual life – an annual Jesuit retreat, weekly confession, and bi-weekly mass and communion.[32] Frequent visits to the Blessed Sacrament, von Hügel insisted, gave him greater peace than he would otherwise have had. His diaries frequently include the word 'Visit', indicating this practice. The Benedictine monk Cuthbert Butler described his walks with von Hügel. They would be discussing all manner of spiritual topics when von Hügel would suddenly excuse himself, enter a Catholic church and be suddenly rapt in prayerful awe before the Blessed Sacrament; those who hadn't seen this side of him knew only 'half the man'.[33]

Another lifelong practice was daily spiritual reading. *The Imitation of Christ*, the *Confessions* of St Augustine, the Psalms and the Gospels were the main texts von Hügel read and digested. He tried to 'live' the *Confessions* at their deepest for fifty years,[34] and was constantly aware of wanting to learn from the great minds of the past. He believed that, standing on their shoulders, he would be able to see further than they did, but that on his own feet he would see less far than they saw.[35]

Formation through Abbé Huvelin

The most significant influence on von Hügel's spiritual formation was his spiritual director, the Parisian priest Abbé Henri Huvelin. Von Hügel described Abbé Huvelin as the 'deepest and most salutary influence' on him of anyone he knew in the flesh.[36] He emphatically declared that he owed more to Huvelin than anyone else he'd ever known: 'I learnt all that I know from Huvelin.'[37] Though this is clearly hyperbolic, von Hügel was substantially formed through twenty-six years of spiritual direction from Huvelin and his saintly example.

Abbé Huvelin (1838–1910) was one of the pre-eminent spiritual directors of the nineteenth century, and many came to him for spiritual counsel, including Charles de Foucauld. People queued outside Huvelin's door daily where he received visitors from two to five each afternoon. The main record of his spiritual nurture of the Baron is contained in sixteen letters and a series of 'Sayings', made during two week-long visits in 1886 and 1893. Von Hügel often sent these 'Sayings' to spiritual directees, describing them as 'winged words and fiery darts' by an individual with 'spiritual greatness and piercing vision', from a life penetrated by God.[38] But, more than his words, it was who Huvelin was that had an impact on the Baron: '*There* sanctity stood before me in the flesh.'[39] Von Hügel's descriptions of Huvelin's 'sanctity' provide us with a portrait: a 'spiritually aboundingly healthful, mystical saint'; a 'tonic tenderness'; holiness, radiating joy; a 'deep and heroic' personality, whose selfless love brought comfort to countless troubled souls.[40]

Humility was a recurring theme in Huvelin's teaching, summed up in the necessity of three glances: one in awareness of our sinfulness, one towards God begging for mercy, and one towards our neighbours to both forgive and bless.[41] He recognized that we must respect the 'type' that God is forming, for God is the 'true' director of souls. Huvelin attended to von Hügel's intensity, repeatedly encouraging him to silence, to rest and to take things more quietly.[42] He ushered the Baron into the company of seventeenth-century French scholar-saints like Jean Grou and François Fénelon, so that he could learn from how they alternated work and prayer.[43] Huvelin believed that God saves us through souls before us who have received the spiritual life and then pass it on, out of their love for us.[44] Huvelin's legacy was passed on to von Hügel's spiritual directees, including Evelyn Underhill, who highlighted the Abbé's supernatural ability to read souls.[45]

The Baron's context

Von Hügel engaged in the Catholic modernist cause between 1890 and 1909, and some commentators believe that this involvement had a residual impact on his later spiritual direction. Lawrence Barmann argues that any research into von Hügel's spirituality needs to be grounded in the Baron's identity as a modernist as the framework for his 'lived faith'.[46] His 'three elements of religion' were partly a response to issues raised by modernism – that the Catholic Church of the time reduced religion to spiritual experience alone, independent of theology or of the discipline of institutional practice. However, von Hügel made it clear that his involvement in modernism ended in 1909, and that his writings since that 'definitely closed period' had moved on from the earlier orientation.[47]

During the first two decades of the twentieth century in Britain, idealistic immanentism – 'God in us' – was manifest. Reginald John Campbell's book, *The New Theology* (1907) was a vivid illustration of this trend: 'my God is my deeper self, and yours too.'[48] This doctrine of divine immanence challenged previous understandings of transcendence. Immanentism was viewed by von Hügel as a great danger, and his writings were a 'passionate protest' against it.[49] He also had a horror of pantheism, convinced that it leaves no space for contrition, humility or adoration because it allows no room for sin or for God; he believed that we 'escape' pantheism through Christ.[50] Von Hügel responded to the growing threat of pantheism by emphasizing the ontological difference between God and humanity and, consequently, the place of a true sense of transcendence. He reacted to modernist immanentism with a 'transcendent immanentism' – something we 'do not make but find'.[51] In so doing, he recovered for the Anglo-Saxon religious world a sense of transcendence and corrected a strain of 'subjectively-tilted psychologism' in liberal religion.[52]

In reaction to the subjectivism and projectionism of his day, the Baron highlighted the given reality of God. He believed it made a massive difference whether we approach religion rejoicing in 'realities distinct from ourselves', or with subjectivist understandings.[53] He emphasized a realist philosophy, stressing the 'given, is-ness' of God, which was one of his unique contributions to religious thought.[54] He also countered projectionism with scientific observation of traces of God, encouraging his directees to observe and see God at work.

The first two decades of the twentieth century also saw a resurgence of interest in spirituality and mysticism. Von Hügel largely valued this reaction to rationalism, with its emphasis on intuition, feeling and the heart. But along with this shift came a rise in spiritualism. He viewed the fascination with theosophy and spiritualism as a reaction to an over-focus on the intellectual element of religion.[55] Von Hügel's diaries document his loathing of these secular spiritualities. Evelyn Underhill recalled how the Baron 'abhorred' anything with a pantheistic or unitarian trend.[56] Given the openness to supernatural phenomena in his day, von Hügel received many letters from people concerning supernatural phenomena: 'angelic apparitions', 'spiritualism' and 'reincarnation'.[57] His neighbours, the Garceaus, asked the Baron to meet a princess who was a spiritualist but he refused, stating that he was the 'least spiritualistic' of men and that it left him 'absolutely uninterested'.[58]

The Victorian world view was shattered by the First World War. Discussions about divine immanence and transcendence largely came to a halt when war began, as England became more secular. Suddenly the problems of evil and suffering were more pressing issues. During the war, von Hügel, with his German accent, dark trench coat and habit of scurrying over hills with a geological hammer, was sometimes viewed as an enemy alien.[59] On the day Britain declared war on Austria, the Baron gave up his Austrian citizenship and was naturalized a British citizen.

Published works

In 1908, when von Hügel was fifty-six, his first book, *The Mystical Element of Religion*, was published, in which he used his biographical study of the pre-Reformation married saint, Catherine of Genoa, to examine mysticism. He wanted to scrutinize closely a soul of spiritual depth that presented the 'helps, problems and dangers' of the mystical spirit.[60] He also endeavoured to discover how a soul like Catherine's, with a developed taste for God, could still make room for the historical, institutional and intellectual elements in her religious life.[61] Writing this book had a profoundly humbling effect on the Baron, and William Temple described the text as the most important theological work written in English in the first half of the twentieth century.[62] The Baron's second book, *Eternal Life*, was published in 1912, followed by *The German Soul* in 1916. *Eternal Life* had begun as an article but von Hügel became so engrossed in his subject that his composition grew. For financial reasons, he chose to have eleven of his papers compiled into the volume *Essays and Addresses on the Philosophy of Religion, First Series*, in 1921. His final years were spent working on *The Reality of God*. Von Hügel's daughter Hildegard described this as a 'beloved' book which he strained every nerve to complete, even dictating to his secretary the night before his death.[63] In the unfinished text, von Hügel declared it was only in the last few years that he had found 'clearness' concerning the roots of faith.[64] All of von Hügel's published works are the reflections of a mature thinker, mainly during his final decade.

Several of the works were published posthumously: *Essays and Addresses on the Philosophy of Religion, Second Series* (1926), *Selected Letters* (1927), *Letters from Baron Friedrich von Hügel to a Niece* (1928), *Some Notes on the Petrine Claims* (1930) and *The Reality of God and Religion and Agnosticism* (1931). Von Hügel's literary remains, along with his earlier unfinished writings about Sir Alfred Lyall, were brought together for this final publication. Von Hügel found in Lyall an agnostic soul with a spirit hungering after the invisible, the eternal.[65] The Baron's openness to explore the spirituality of Lyall's agnosticism reveals von Hügel's own secure love of God at the centre, which gave him the freedom to explore the periphery. In addition to these published volumes, von Hügel wrote many articles and some reviews.[66]

Von Hügel's writing style has been criticized for its long sentences, over-elaboration and obscurity, which the Baron attributed to his fluency in several languages and his German blood.[67] Yet at times his writing bursts forth with flashes of brilliant, concise epigrams and original, memorable metaphors.[68] The Scottish philosopher Norman Kemp Smith described von Hügel's writings as the 'outcome' of a life's rich experience.[69] While Maude Petre recognized the greatness of his writings, she acknowledged that his character and presence were far greater.[70] Canon Lillie similarly highlighted the Baron's intense, rich personal life which penetrates his writings, making them 'glow'.[71] Von Hügel himself spoke of the necessity of 'quiet listening to the heartbeat of real life' and 'genuine, gentle receptivity' for writing to be effective.[72]

Family life

In 1873, at the age of twenty-one, von Hügel married Lady Mary Herbert. The Anglican Herberts of Pembroke didn't consider von Hügel to be good enough for Mary, on the grounds of class and religion. The Baron wrote to Mary of his disappointment at entering a family 'at best tolerated'.[73] Even those who had married into the Herbert fold didn't approve of him. Arthur Ponsonby believed that von Hügel could convincingly argue that black is white, while the composer Hubert Parry described the Baron as unimpressive on acquaintance.[74] However, following their marriage, von Hügel told his new wife that he'd never dreamed of such happiness.[75] Despite his dubious welcome, marrying into the Herbert family opened doors in British aristocratic circles for the Baron.

In 1876 the young couple settled in London, living at 4 Holford Road, Hampstead, before moving in 1903 to 13 Vicarage Gate, Kensington. Their proximity to Hampstead Heath and Kensington Gardens enabled the Baron to take daily afternoon walks with his Pekingese dog. He bestowed great affection on his dogs, and Puck was always given the best chair.[76] His dogs stood in relation to their master in an analogous way to how humanity stands to God, hence providing material for many spiritual lessons.[77] Von Hügel's love for Puck was evident when the dog had to be put down in 1922: he had 'lain looking' at the Baron with 'deep love and perfect confidence till his eyes broke'.[78]

Von Hügel was a devoted father to his three daughters, Gertrud, Hildegard and Thekla. Given that the majority of his directees were female, fathering three girls was valuable preparation for closely relating to women. Von Hügel managed his daughters' education himself, teaching them the catechism, history and languages. He set them twice-yearly examinations which friends described as more difficult than those at the universities.[79] Perspectives on von Hügel's fathering are best provided by his daughters. Hildegard, the least academic of the three, commented that throughout her life her father took the greatest interest in whatever interested her, despite these being outside his own interests: 'he loved to play with us', teaching them about trees, birds and animals on his constant walks with them.[80] Thekla, an enclosed Carmelite nun, described him as a 'devoted father' who took 'every pain' to bring them up well, his one longing being for 'God alone'.[81]

The Baron's daughter who was closest to him, Gertrud, died in 1915. It was a defining moment for von Hügel. For months he had prayed in churches in Rome, waiting on God's will in submission beside the deathbed of the 'dearest being in his world'.[82] Gertrud's death was the turning point where von Hügel left modernism behind, and became focused on the central truths of life and death.[83] The pain of Gertrud's death was exacerbated by the Baron's feeling of responsibility that sharing his doubts and questions had led Gertrud into a spiritual crisis lasting several years. However, during her final days, von Hügel observed with relief her childlike faith and deep peace. Following Gertrud's death, von Hügel's niece Gwendolen Greene became the person the Baron most nurtured spiritually. In 1921 he told Gwen that he had not tried to care and serve and 'feed any soul' as much as hers.[84]

Juliet Mansel, a teenage girl who lived for a while with the von Hügels, described the unique atmosphere at Vicarage Gate: the warmth, humour and tolerance towards the many diverse people who visited the house, whether men of learning for the Baron or musicians for Lady Mary.[85] This is echoed by Frances Lillie, another spiritual directee, who depicted the von Hügels as a devoted and united family.[86] However, at one point there is an indication that Mary felt threatened by the Baron's attention to women receiving his spiritual direction. The Baron reassured her that his friendship with the women was in origin and essence 'wholesome, useful, loyal to you and to all . . . I am interested in and, please God, helpful to . . . kittle-cattle souls'.[87]

Friendships

Von Hügel's diaries reveal that he wrote many letters to friends. He described letter writing as a 'specially blest' way of maintaining 'precious touch' with friends.[88] One of the by-products of his partial deafness was that letter writing became his primary vehicle for spiritual direction, and his letters provide us with an unusually complete record of his direction. Personal letters can provide some of the most revealing expressions of the soul.

While living in Hampstead, von Hügel saw a walk on the Heath, or later in Kensington Gardens or Hyde Park, as the best setting for talking about matters of spiritual depth. In addition to his daily afternoon walks, he had a steady stream of visitors because of his special gift for friendship. The Oxford philosopher C. C. J. Webb 'reverenced' the Baron above all living souls, describing their friendship as one of the chief blessings of his life.[89]

The Baron recognized the necessity of engaging with living thinkers, for the dead cannot help us to develop in the same way, hence he told the philosopher Norman Kemp Smith that nothing 'makes one grow' more than engaging with friends we respect.[90] He enjoyed friends from many ecumenical backgrounds, including Cardinal John Henry Newman, who influenced him towards his 'three elements of religion' through his preface to the third edition of his *Via Media*. Evelyn Underhill observed that the Baron left no one 'unchanged' by his friendship.[91]

Evelyn Underhill's description of the Baron

One of the most vivid pictures of the Baron is provided by Evelyn Underhill. She believed that his ability to hold together and to practise the pastoral and philosophic sides of the spiritual life made him the 'most influential religious personality' of her time.[92] She described his 'immense spiritual transcendency' as an 'Alpine quality'.[93] Personal interaction with him was like encountering a 'volcanic mountain' because he combined a 'rock-like faith' and 'massive' intellect with an 'incandescent fervour – the hidden fires' of his intense interior life. She described his 'piercing black eyes which compelled truth and obtained it' and the 'awe and passion' she felt when he uttered the name of God.[94] Evelyn described him as full of the 'breadth', 'depth' and 'tenderness' of the saints, and

15

possessed of a 'spiritual creativeness' and capacity for penetrating and 'vivifying' souls.[95] Thinker, prophet, contemplative and father of souls – all these aspects of his life existed in such 'close union' that each couldn't be understood unless considered as part of the whole.[96]

Evelyn also portrayed the Baron as a 'lovable old man', a 'saint transfigured by his passionate sense of God', full of 'unhurried interest' in humble people and homely amusements, remarking with complete simplicity of a disappointment, 'Another little humiliation for me – what a good thing!'[97] She described von Hügel rescuing many from the darkness of intellectual entanglements through his own 'unique method'.[98] Directees were saved from 'theological suicide' through his dislike of 'strain and excess' in relation to doctrinal problems, and his encouragement that people feed their souls on the great truths they *can* see.[99] His main interest lay in souls, in helping them to grow and in 'arousing' the human response to the reality, richness and attraction of God, to which end he 'valued, many diverse means'.[100]

Personal accolades

Following von Hügel's death, his wife, Mary, received endless letters from spiritual directees speaking of his profound influence on their lives. One woman wrote that he had taught her all that seemed 'worth knowing', and she highlighted his unique 'deep insight, sympathy and comprehension', plus his 'profound piety and devotion'.[101] Another wrote that she owed him everything she most valued, and another that he had 'cured' her soul of sickness.[102]

The impact of von Hügel's public utterances were reported by several people. His brother Anatole observed a young mechanic and his wife who sat motionless in an uncomfortable position during a long lecture von Hügel gave, their eyes never leaving his face while he talked about deep truths.[103] Similarly, an Aussie bushman who had listened to von Hügel exclaimed that, even though he didn't understand a word he said, he could sit and listen to him for a week.[104] A friend of Hildegard's recalled talking with von Hügel – his 'beauty and ripe wisdom' and 'generous outpouring' never left her.[105] After von Hügel's death, on several occasions during LSSR discussions, someone would quote him and, whatever he had said, the Society would 'all accept [it] . . . so strong was the impact of this genius . . . Wherever he went, he seemed to produce that effect'.[106]

The Swedish archbishop Nathan Söderblom described von Hügel as someone to whom he 'owe[d] so much in spiritual things'.[107] He stated that no one else in his time had been such a 'teacher and an initiator to seeking and believing souls [*sic*]' for all sections of the Church than the Baron, for he was a 'model and teacher' to many from different denominations.[108] Maude Petre described von Hügel as 'a great liberator' opening doors for imprisoned souls, and his death made her feel that a piece of life had been 'hacked out'; an 'Alpine range' had 'disappeared'.[109]

Another window on von Hügel was provided by his sister-in-law Isy, who viewed his body after his death and described his face looking:

> as if transfigured by something that had come as the spirit passed; there is no other word than transfiguration – absolute peace – and life shining not on but through . . . When one came back to him the strange look still was there – immovable yet living. Everyone felt a great wonder of spiritual beauty.[110]

Von Hügel was buried beside his mother and sister at Downside Abbey in Bath. Huvelin's motto was the verse von Hügel chose for the inscription on his headstone: 'What have I in heaven but thee, and besides Thee what do I desire on earth?'[111]

Having had a taste of the Baron's narrative and context, we now turn to sketch Evelyn Underhill's story, focusing primarily on aspects that were relevant to her spiritual formation.

2

Introducing Evelyn Underhill

> One torch lights another . . . It is best to learn from others; it
> gives a touch of creatureliness.[1]
> (von Hügel)

Evelyn Underhill was one of the most widely read writers of spirituality in the first half of the twentieth century. Her life story has
already been told in the biographies of Lucy Menzies (unpublished),
Margaret Cropper, Christopher Armstrong and Dana Greene.[2] Her
close friends described her 'fascinating', 'complex' and 'elusive' personality, as faithfully portrayed in Armstrong's biography.[3] Here
we simply highlight some aspects of Evelyn's narrative that had an
impact on her spiritual formation.

Formation through home and formal education

Evelyn Underhill was born on 6 December 1875 in Wolverhampton,
England. Soon after her birth, the family moved to London, where
her father worked as a barrister. The family motto – *Vive et Ama*
(Live and Love) – was embossed on the family notepaper. Evelyn
appears to have had a loving childhood, though as she was a single
child it must have been a lonely one.

When young, Evelyn experienced sudden fainting fits and
lamented that she never had any real education owing to this ill
health.[4] Her mother taught her at home, then she attended boarding
school at Sandgate House, near Folkestone, from the age of thirteen
to sixteen. Letters reveal Evelyn pleading with her mother not to
make her the last child collected at the end of term.[5] Their lack of

closeness was revealed when von Hügel highlighted their differing outlooks as exacerbating Evelyn's grief after her mother's death.[6]

Though she declared that she 'wasn't brought up' on religion, school chapel services provided her with some questionable religious formation, such as her preparation for Anglican confirmation, which began, 'My child, your life hitherto has been one continuous Sin, and you are now walking on the brink of Hell.'[7] Similarly, Evelyn described a sermon about Satan by the school chaplain, who spoke as though he'd seen him.[8]

At the age of fifteen, Evelyn had a black notebook where she wrote down prayers, hymns and self-examination. Though lively and talented, she was also introspective and self-deprecating, recording nineteen sins including selfishness, pride and self-deceit; but Armstrong indicates that her adolescent scrapbook, letters and black notebook provide the impression of more positive attributes, such as her being sensitive, open, witty, self-aware and loving.[9]

On the eve of her seventeenth birthday, Evelyn wrote that if we are to see God it will be through nature and humanity.[10] She also recorded her desire to be an author so she could 'influence' people, adding that she hoped her mind would 'not grow tall to look down on things but wide to embrace all sorts of things'.[11] This desire for open expansiveness became a mark of her life and spirituality.

In 1893 Evelyn studied botany, history, languages and art at the Ladies' Department of King's College, London, where she gained a competence in foreign languages, an enhanced love of nature and art skills. Later she studied philosophy at home, using her father's library. Philosophy brought her to an 'intelligent and irresponsible' theism, but it was her encounter with Italian religious art that brought her closer to the infinite.[12]

Formation through Italian religious art

Italy stirred Evelyn's fascination with the mystical. For a decade, from 1898, she went on yearly trips there with her mother. She viewed Italy as the 'holy land of Europe' and as 'medicinal to the soul', believing that a certain type of mind must go there to 'find itself'.[13] Italian art helped Evelyn gradually and unconsciously grow 'into an understanding of things'.[14] These Italian trips were deeply formative, drawing her towards the unseen reality. She began to encounter the religion behind the art, linking the natural and the supernatural. Through religious architecture and art, Evelyn encountered beauty in a way that made her long for the divine. She described a particular chapel as having close communion between the supernatural and the 'actual structure of the earth', and another as 'soaked' with a 'sense of prayer and adoration'.[15] In particular, the frescos of Fra Angelico, such as *The Last Supper*, *The Mocking of Christ* and *Crucifixion and Saints*, made a strong impression on Evelyn, causing her to reflect on the person of Christ. Accounts of her journeys and responses from 1901 to 1907 are outlined in Evelyn's *Shrines and Cities of France and Italy* (1949).

Throughout these years, Evelyn was courting her childhood friend and neighbour Hubert Stuart Moore. However, as her world enlarged spiritually, she became guarded about sharing her photographs of religious subjects with him because he had mocked such things in the past.[16] Despite this, in 1904 Hubert demonstrated his pride in Evelyn's pursuits when he collected eighty reviews of her first novel, *The Grey World*. The central theme of this novel was beauty providing access to the invisible realm. The protagonist, Willie, visits Roman Catholic churches in Italy, gazes at creation and reads poetry and mystical writings, and thereby gains access to the world beyond. Evelyn wrote two more novels in 1907 and 1909, attempting to show eternal things through and in the temporal.[17] But, despite her apprehension of the supernatural through art, she was still seeking and exploring and was gradually drawn into the occult.

Formation through the Golden Dawn

Around 1903 Evelyn joined an occult brotherhood called the

Hermetic Society of the Golden Dawn. The three founders of this order were Freemasons and Evelyn was given the occultist pseudonym *Soror Quaerens Lucem* (the sister seeking enlightenment). It was the type of society that someone interested in the 'metaphysico-mystical scene' of the day, yet not connected to churches, would have felt drawn to, for it emphasized encounter with ultimate realities through 'incantations and rituals' from various sources.[18] Evelyn participated in these rituals in an attempt to experience the invisible, supernatural world beyond the senses. By the end of 1905, she had progressed to the stage of sitting the exam for the lower grade of the Outer Order brotherhood,[19] but gradually the shine wore off and she withdrew from the group some time around 1906. In her words, this 'irresponsible' period 'did not last long'.[20] However, this period in Evelyn's life was echoed in her ongoing valuing of rituals, later transferred to Christianity – 'the magic chain' of 'congregational worship', 'sacraments and symbols'.[21]

Formation through a Catholic retreat

A year or so after Evelyn's emergence from the Golden Dawn, she became engaged to Hubert Stuart Moore. During that year, Evelyn and her next-door neighbour Ethel Barker secretly went on a retreat at the Franciscan Convent of Perpetual Adoration at Southampton. On the fourth day Evelyn left, fearful that she might hastily decide to convert. For 'gradually the net closed in' and she was 'driven nearer and nearer to Christianity', half of her 'wishing' it was 'true' but half 'resisting violently'.[22] The following day at home, Evelyn was, in her words, 'converted, quite suddenly, once and for all by an overpowering vision which had really no specifically Christian elements' but which 'convinced' her that the Catholic religion was 'true'; she thought Catholicism would be her 'ultimate home'.[23] Her friend Ethel converted, leaving Evelyn in a quandary as to whether to join her.

Evelyn wrote to Father Benson that she'd come 'half-way' from agnosticism to Catholicism but was 'unable to get farther'.[24] By April

1907 she had made up her mind to be received into the Church. However, her fiancé, Hubert, was heartbroken and vehemently opposed it, fearful that the intimacy of the confessional would affect their impending marriage. He begged her to wait another year and Ethel urged Evelyn not to break off the engagement.[25] However loath Evelyn was to give up her desire to convert, she loved Hubert and would not sacrifice her 'domestic happiness'.[26] Hubert's opposition, coupled with the Catholic modernist crisis, halted her intention. The papal encyclical *Pascendi Dominici Gregis*, which condemned modernism, terminated the discussions she was having with Father Benson, for she considered herself a 'modernist', and the 'suppressions and evasions' now imposed on Catholics made her conversion impossible; she would not give up her 'intellectual liberty' or endure the suppressions that were being imposed.[27] Her decision against conversion was pivotal for her future vocation as an Anglican retreat leader.

It must have been unsettling for Evelyn when Ethel wrote later that year saying that Sister Eucharistie had said that Evelyn was ready to be received and was in some ways much more Catholic than Ethel.[28] Still restless, in early 1909 Evelyn reinitiated a short correspondence with Father Benson. She was concerned about whether her 'flame of adoration' could keep burning bright without the sacraments; moreover she was perturbed about self-deception and 'interior dereliction' in prayer, wondering if her experiences were a 'hypnotic trick'.[29] Benson diagnosed her sudden 'blankness' as the result of not being 'planted' in the 'soil' of organized religious life.[30] But Evelyn felt unable to find a church, rejecting Rome's 'narrow exclusiveness' but also unable to accept Anglicanism, lamenting, 'I do miss churches when I have not got them to run to'.[31] She ended her correspondence with Benson, feeling that she was wasting his time discussing her 'internal uproar'. A greater man than Benson was required to help her troubled soul.[32]

Formation through marriage

Evelyn married Hubert in July 1907 and they moved into 50 Campden Hill Square, London. This eighteenth-century terraced house, opposite a quiet, leafy public garden was to be their home for most of their married life. Evelyn gradually settled into her new married routine. Each morning Hubert left early for his work as a barrister, returning at six p.m. each evening. Evelyn organized domestic duties with two servants before ten in the morning. Her housemaid recalls how she treated them like family, helping them in many ways.[33] As an Edwardian woman of relative leisure, as was appropriate for her class, Evelyn wrote until lunch, making it a rule not to be interrupted between ten and one, then often had lunch with her mother; afternoons were frequently spent receiving visitors at home.[34] Any friend or 'case' with whom she was still talking at six would tactfully depart once Hubert arrived home, leaving their evenings free.[35] Evelyn also met people for tea, attended Benediction at the Chapel of the Assumption and visited the poor through the Health Society and the Poor Law.[36] The Stuart Moores belonged to the Kensington Music Club and the Cantata Club, though Evelyn spent most evenings writing letters on her knee by the fire.[37]

The drawing room and dining room were on the ground floor, but Evelyn had her own study on the first floor, which was decorated in purple, blue and silver hues and lined with books from floor to ceiling.[38] On her study mantelpiece sat a plaque embroidered with the word ETERNITY, which was sometimes placed on her writing desk.[39] This had been given to her by a gardening friend in 1916, who had found it in an antique shop and had then embroidered the word. It became a treasured reminder to Evelyn that eternity could be experienced now. She wanted to be perpetually reminded of the invisible, unseen reality lying behind her visible world. In her study she often knelt to write – 'half-praying, half-writing' – when alone.[40]

Though more aware of the unseen than most people, Evelyn was also 'passionately appreciative' of the seen.[41] Beautiful objects surrounded her as both sets of parents were collectors of silver, glass and china, and her mother also collected lace. Evelyn was also fond of elegant clothes and was always tastefully dressed, sometimes in a little Flemish lace cap, which was symbolic of her detachment from worldly opinion.[42] She was hospitable, often entertaining friends and acquaintances. Also friendly with their neighbours, she encouraged everyone at Campden Hill Square to put lights in their windows each Christmas to 'welcome the Christ Child'.[43]

As a keen gardener, Evelyn was tender-hearted towards all growing things. Once, when arranging flowers, she stopped Lucy Menzies throwing some withered flowers into the fire, saying that it would be 'cruel'.[44] Gardening took up much of Evelyn's 'play hours' for she adored flowers, particularly snowdrops and larkspur.[45] She was always a lover of cats, and when she was made a fellow of King's College, the Dean spoke of how she 'enlivened her leisure' through talking to cats.[46]

Evelyn appreciated beauty and aesthetics. Whether it was autumn hats in Paris, the early morning light on mountains in Avila or the Perugian landscape soaked in light, her senses were alert to the wonder of creation.[47] Seeing harvest fields made her feel 'sort of wild' and inhaling the fragrance of country violets was a 'perfect joy'.[48] While leading retreats, she noticed birdsong intermingling with hymns, and one Easter she found 'soaking' in the trees and flowers more 'spiritually suggestive' than her previous experiences of ecclesiasticism.[49]

By all accounts, the Stuart Moores had a happy marriage. When she was once asked if she had any children Evelyn replied, 'Alas, no, my dears, only cats.'[50] Her playful and affectionate nature is revealed in her closing words in letters to Hubert, for example, from your 'mad bad wife who thinks of you all the time'.[51] Though Hubert had no interest in religion, he gladly drove his wife to church at the Chapel of the Assumption in Kensington Square and sympathized as much as he could with all that she did. Menzies described them as an 'ideally happy couple', where law and religion lived 'peacefully together'.[52] They shared interests such as bookbinding and making weekly excursions in their Baby Austin, named Augustine, and later in their larger Austin called Monica.[53] Evelyn loved the countryside deeply, and they escaped there whenever possible.

Despite her cheerfulness, Evelyn led an inwardly lonely life between 1907 and 1921.[54] While she was tenderly affectionate towards her husband and her parents, they didn't understand her inner life, so she kept her 'secret stress' and 'spiritual troubles' to herself.[55] Part of this inward strain came from living in the 'borderland' without a church home for fourteen years. Evelyn struggled to work out how to maintain contact with the Church when she was not actually a member of it, so she threw herself into writing about the Christian mystics, who she believed lived mainly independent of any religious affiliation.[56]

Formation through early contact with the Baron

Keeping company with the medieval mystics expanded Evelyn's whole being. She began writing *Mysticism* in 1907 and it was published in 1911. Her methodology took her beyond her 'scraps of experience', so she also had to rely on her 'sympathetic imagination', which she recognized as 'not always safe'.[57] Despite this, *Mysticism* was well received, establishing her as an expert on the subject. Evelyn sent von Hügel her book, inscribed: 'offered with gratitude and deep respect by the writer'.[58] Three days later, von Hügel invited Evelyn to his home to discuss it.[59] He was an authority in mysticism, having published his two-volume *The Mystical Element of Religion*. Evelyn had read this work, which the Baron had sent her, acknowledging it in her Foreword as a 'constant source of stimulus and encouragement' while writing *Mysticism*.[60]

When discussing *Mysticism*, the Baron had some suggestions about how to improve it for its reprint. He criticized its lack of attention to institutional, historical religion and its insufficient emphasis on the gap between Creator and creature.[61] Evelyn ignored his offer to revise her work over the period of a month, but after the Baron's death she undertook a serious revision of *Mysticism*, adhering to this early advice in her Introduction. She wrote then that if she were planning the book now, she would have emphasized the 'paradox of utter contrast yet profound relation' between Creator and creature and the 'predominant part' in our formation played by the 'free and prevenient action of the Supernatural . . . by grace'.[62] She also included additional quotes from St Paul and the New Testament, replacing those on alchemy by A. E. Waite.

Two months after meeting the Baron, Evelyn wrote to a friend:

I have become the friend (or rather the disciple and admirer) of von Hügel. He is the most wonderful personality I have ever known – so saintly, so truthful, sane and tolerant. I feel safe and happy sitting in his shadow.[63]

Over the following decade the Baron nurtured Evelyn, who was twenty-three years his junior, in a fatherly manner, through ongoing contact, as evidenced in her warm inscriptions when she sent him books. In 1911 he told Evelyn that his general rule with people like her, who were non-Catholic, was to 'feed' and encourage any Catholic instincts and practices 'already active or near to birth' and let them feel the 'depth and tenderness and heroism of Christian sanctity greater and richer than . . . found elsewhere', and to leave their souls to 'God's ways'.[64] Evelyn valued the Baron's sensitivity and caution, qualities that had developed in him through his years of escaping condemnation as a Catholic modernist.[65]

Von Hügel mentioned Evelyn in his diaries. For instance, in 1912, he answered her questions about 'N. T. Mysticism', then delivered written articles to her the following day.[66] In 1913 Evelyn sent him *The Mystic Way*, inscribed with 'the writer's deepest respect: a small mark of gratitude for the inestimable benefits which she has received from his generous help, his personal sympathy, and his published work'.[67] Von Hügel read Evelyn's book and wrote her an encouraging note, saying how 'carefully' she had 'borne in mind the all-important place and function in religion of liturgical acts, of the Sacrament, of the Visible, of History'.[68] Evelyn had a long talk with him about her book. He supported it, though he felt she had not gone 'so far' as he thought she 'should have done', perhaps indicating that they had talked about the book while it was being written.[69] Evelyn recounted his 'firm but gentle lecture' on her 'Quakerish leanings!' He believed that 'such interior religion' is fine for our 'exalted moments' but is not useful for the ordinary 'dull jog-trot of daily life', and is thus not a 'whole religion' as we are not simply 'pure spirit'. He likened a 'steady-going parish priest' to a cosy 'eiderdown', who was yet a 'better standby for daily life than any prophet'.[70] Evelyn found it 'hard and dreary' doctrine but wasn't prepared to say it was wrong; she later viewed her book as 'too immanentist'.[71]

Formation through the mystics

During these years, Evelyn was a 'painstaking' and 'understanding champion' of the mystics.[72] By 1914 a mystical revival was under way. A reaction to the material success of the Victorian age meant that people were becoming introspective and focusing on first-hand experience.[73] Through Evelyn, the mystics became more widely known in accessible paperback editions with clear introductions.

Evelyn was not simply a mystical theologian but a mystic who wrote from her experiences. While she was especially appreciative of St John of the Cross, she was also deeply influenced by St Teresa of Ávila, Jean-Pierre de Caussade, Francis de Sales, François Fénelon, Abbé Henri de Tourville, and Abbé Henri Huvelin. Over the years she wrote many biographical studies of mystics, such as John van Ruysbroeck and Jacopone da Todi, and edited volumes including *The Cloud of Unknowing* and Walter Hilton's *The Scale of Perfection*.

Her book *Practical Mysticism* (1914) made mysticism accessible to ordinary people. *The Mystics of the Church* (1925) was her final book on mysticism. She then segued into writing about the spiritual life for lay people, the focus of her final two decades. Earlier on, she had also written two books about spirituality under the pseudonym John Cordelier.

Evelyn also published two volumes of poetry – *Immanence* (1912) and *Theophanies* (1916) – but stopped writing poetry because it was 'too easy'.[74] Nature was a revelation of the divine for Evelyn, though some critiqued her poetry as immanentist and pantheistic. The first lines of 'Immanence' reveal her approach:

> I come in the little things,
> Saith the Lord . . . I have set my feet
> Amidst the delicate and bladed wheat . . .[75]

Evelyn also helped translate poetry and was thus influenced by non-Christian mystics. In 1913, when Rabindranath Tagore was convalescing in London, Evelyn worked with him to translate poetry by Kabir, a fifteenth-century Hindu mystical poet. She described Tagore as her 'beloved Indian Prophet', a 'master' in the things she cared for but knew little about, viewing Kabir's poems as a 'priceless possession'.[76] Evelyn's openness to non-Christian mystics was also reflected in her later inclusion of a prayer by a Sufi mystic, Rabia al-Basri, in her Prayer Book for retreat leading.[77] But if she was ever tempted to a superficial syncretism, her spiritual intuition and von Hügel's influence held her back.

Formation through the suffering of war

Not many letters or documents relating to Evelyn remain from 1914–1918 because of the disruptive war years. As Evelyn was about to publish *Practical Mysticism*, war broke out, hence her dedication 'To the Unseen Future'. The Baron was sent a copy inscribed 'with deepest respect and very kind regards from his friend and grateful pupil, the writer'; he viewed the text as one of Evelyn's 'excessively mystical' works.[78]

During the war Evelyn worked in Naval Intelligence preparing and translating guidebooks. But even during the horrors of war she was capable of lightheartedness. A colleague recalled her as a 'small-ish, stooping' woman with an animated face 'creased with laughter and twinkling with fun'.[79] Evelyn cheekily compiled a guidebook to an imaginary place, complete with fauna and flora. It was sent to the head of the department, who read it and was about to have it printed when something struck him as 'odd'.[80]

In June 1916 von Hügel wrote to Evelyn, having just read her book review in the *Harvard Theological Review*.[81] He described her review as 'strongly insistent on the value of the historical element in Christianity' and on the 'danger' of subordinating the 'historical to the symbolical or mystical interpretation of formu-laries'.[82] He saw this as 'most satisfactory', adding:

> I have long felt how large is your public – how many souls will be led right or wrong by yourself, with your rare charm of style, large knowledge of literature, and delicate interest-ingness of character . . . I rejoice, I believe more fully than if I discovered some growth in myself – for you can and do reach more people than I can ever expect to reach myself.[83]

His letter closed with an invitation to his talk on 'Heaven and Hell', followed by a joyful sign-off: 'Yours v. sincerely and delightedly'. He wrote another letter in 1916 saying he was glad that Evelyn held to the principle 'from God to immortality', and not vice versa.[84]

But, despite these signs of 'growth' observed by the Baron, 1917 was a year of suffering for Evelyn, and she wrote little. The trauma of war was close at hand through the bombing and destruction of the house next door to her parents'. More significantly, her two cousins were killed at the front and Ethel Barker became terminally ill.[85] During this season Evelyn experienced an increasingly 'anti-institutional bias', drifting towards 'inwardness'.[86] She described the abnormal conditions of the war years as 'bad' for spiritual lives, confessing that 'most of us are failing badly', for detachment is 'almost impossible': transcending the here and now demands a 'strength of will and a power of withdrawal which very few possess', hence she found spiritual things 'secondary & unreal'.[87] Evelyn told the Baron she 'went to pieces' during this period, for her 'disembodied and abstracted' mysticism was unable to deal with life's 'harsh' realities.[88]

In 1918 there was a shift in Evelyn towards institutional affiliation. In an article, 'The Future of Mysticism', she argued that mysticism 'needs a body' and that, 'divorced' from all institutional expression, it can become 'strange, vague or merely sentimental'.[89] Evelyn was writing biographically when she stated that authentic mystical life 'flourishes best' when it is allied with a 'definite religious faith capable of upholding the mystic during the many periods in which his vision fails him'.[90] She was coming to recognize her deep need for some sort of lived community of faith. In 1920 Evelyn sent the Baron her *Essentials of Mysticism*, inscribed 'with kindest regards and respect of the writer'.[91] Though outwardly she looked successful, she had experienced some troubling war years, when her mysticism had been unable to sustain her.

Formation through von Hügel

In 1921, in mid-life despair, Evelyn sought out von Hügel. She viewed him as 'without exception, the most influential religious personality' and the 'most wonderful example of wisdom, sanctity and depth' her 'generation' was ever 'likely to see'.[91] Evelyn asked him for help concerning her 'spiritual views, practices'.[93] Von Hügel replied that her letter had brought him 'great joy', for he had long been 'hoping and praying' for a 'development' in her, and he told her to never shrink from seeing him because he was busy, as it would be 'nothing but consolation' to 'help' her.[94] As well as assuring her that he would engage in 'persevering prayer' for her spiritual welfare, von Hügel asked her to write a report concerning 'where she stood', then he drew up a 'rough set of rules and proposals'.[95] Evelyn was asked to provide a 'second report' concerning how his proposals 'struck' her, which he 'carefully criticized' with quite extensive 'final advice'.[96] The Baron used to spend a full day carefully reflecting on and praying over Evelyn's six-monthly reports and any changes in her position communicated to him by letter meant that he would 'rearrange', 'add to' and rewrite parts to better meet her 'condition'.[97]

The Baron thoroughly approved of Evelyn's shift from 'pure mysticism' to 'traditional, institutional religion': her visible religion would 'safeguard' her invisible religion, while her invisible religion would give 'freshness and variety' to her visible religion.[98] With that 'growth' he no longer had any 'misgivings' concerning her 'popularity', as long as she remained 'firm', growing in this new direction.[99] The Baron had long recognized Evelyn's influence on others and had hoped she would become more 'harmonious' and 'deep' herself so that she could do 'much pure good' instead of a 'little harm mixed with some good'.[100] Von Hügel designated people like Evelyn as 'Ds' – people 'detached' from any communion – and was wary of their influence.[101]

Von Hügel's spiritual direction of Evelyn was quite different from the ongoing contact he had with other directees, such as his niece Gwendolen Greene, whom he met with in person each week. He directed Evelyn only twice a year via letter, with explicit direction that she read the bi-yearly reports once a month.[102] Evelyn was instructed to write him a report every six months, and he 'purposely' didn't see her in between.[103] This is surprising given that he lived only a short walk from her home. However, Menzies suggests that Evelyn often visited the Baron in between times, for it was such a 'relief' to have someone who truly 'understood' her.[104] In 1922 the Baron noted in his diary that Evelyn 'visited for a talk', but most of the other visits in von Hügel's diaries involve her delivering gifts to him or him delivering a note to her.[105] The majority of Evelyn's visits took place in 1924: to deliver roses, flowers for his birthday and her mother's jigsaw puzzles.[106]

Von Hügel's concerns about Evelyn were discussed in a letter to Gwendolen Greene, where he mentioned a person who had 'read' and 'thought' much and who had begun as a 'Pantheistically inclined Agnostic'. His proposals for Evelyn included thinking of Christ at Holy Communion, visiting the poor and considering the need for a historical institutional religion.[107] Evelyn wanted something 'practical' to hold on to, so she summarized von Hügel's advice in a document called 'My Rule', dated Christmas, 1921.[108] It outlined her work with the poor, her spiritual direction work, her prayer life, her mental disposition, the historicity of Christ, her sense stimulations, her spiritual dispositions, her detachment from friendships and her care of those close to her. After only six months of von Hügel's direction, Evelyn reflected that her previous religious life now looked 'thin' and 'solitary'.[109]

The Baron saw real progress in Evelyn's Upton Lectures as 'strongly' and 'self-committingly' aware of the necessity of 'Traditional, Institutional, Sacramental Religion'.[110] In the published version of these talks, *The Life of the Spirit*, Evelyn argued for the necessity of religious institutions for the full life of the Spirit. In the Preface, she described her 'greatest' 'debt' to von Hügel's works, inscribing in the copy she sent him: 'from his unworthy pupil the writer'.[111] In his revised bibliography for the reissue of *The Mystical Element of Religion* (1923), von Hügel mentioned Evelyn's 'interesting progress' from *Mysticism*, which was full of 'charm' but 'lacking the institutional sense', then her 'several excessively mystical' works and finally *The Life of the Spirit*, which was 'bravely insistent upon history and institutionalism, and furnishing a solidly valuable collection of papers'.[112] In 1923 Evelyn sent the Baron her edited edition of *The Scale of Perfection*, inscribed 'from his deeply grateful pupil'.[113]

In that same year, von Hügel thanked Evelyn for her review of his *Mystical Element*, writing, 'I have been written about only by a handful of persons who have really read me; and you have done more than that – have actually lived the chief figures of the long work.'[114] The admiration was mutual. Evelyn was 'deeply aware' of being 'shown by God how to live the right way' through the Baron. Menzies observed how Evelyn was 'desperately serious' about it, both for herself and for the people coming to her for advice, and was 'happy' in the 'way of life' he 'proposed' to her.[115]

Formation through the Church

In early 1921 Evelyn joined the Church of England. Scholars have different theories about why she made this move. Armstrong suggests that Ethel Baker's death in 1921 may have precipitated the shift, while Greene wonders if joining the *Spiritual Entente* influenced this progression.[116] Most obviously, it was the Baron's push towards institutionalism that had precipitated this decision, though the other two influences probably also contributed to the move. A. M. Allchin makes the point that, by coming under von Hügel's direction, Evelyn couldn't help but also be influenced by the Abbé Huvelin. So, ironically, at the point of becoming an Anglican, Evelyn entered into intimate contact with some of the 'deepest' and 'most creative forces' in Roman Catholicism.[117] Though she found being part of the Church challenging, Evelyn argued that criticism of the Church is really criticism of 'ourselves. Were we more spiritually alive, our spiritual homes would be the real nesting-places of new life' – what the Anglican Church gives is the result of what we bring to it.[118] In midsummer 1922, Evelyn wrote to the Baron that she now felt 'quite satisfied' as an Anglican, having discovered a 'corner' she could 'fit into' and people she could 'sympathise' with and work alongside.[119] Attending her first spiritual retreat at Pleshey markedly contributed to this sense of contentment.

Evelyn's spiritual experiences while under the Baron's direction

A unique window into Evelyn's spiritual journey is provided through her spiritual journals. In her 'Green Notebook' (1923–1924), Evelyn recorded that the more vivid her vision of Christ was, the more she could 'escape' her 'maze of self-occupation. He draws, and we run after'.[120] She 'saw and felt' how we are 'in Christ and He in us' – this 'interpenetration of Spirit . . . all of us merged together in Him': the 'all-penetrating Presence of God' through union with Christ.[121] Later she described a 'deep, thrilling-through, comprehensive sense of God – so fully immanent and yet so distinct'. She believed the 'weight' of von Hügel's prayers were 'pressing' her into 'his sort of consciousness'.[122] In 1924 she experienced a 'wonderful golden glow', seeing Jesus, being filled with a 'musical sense of adoration' and smelling a spiritual 'fragrance'; this 'infinite loveliness', 'colour' and 'quiet joy' made her feel '*so* tiny' and 'nothing'.[123] She was being led away from the 'emotional fervour' of her 'chocolate-cream period' to a 'deepening adoration and self-abandonment' through being 'plunged' into an 'Ocean of Love', 'swallowed up – breathless' with a 'formless joy' and 'darkening . . . enlargement' – 'melting into the supreme'.[124]

But she was not always on this spiritual high. Evelyn also mentioned her 'tremendous ups and downs', losing her ability to pray for a time, 'flat' spiritual experiences due to her nerves and her 'humiliating discovery' that she was not as 'surrendered and detached' as she'd hoped.[125] This was the nature of her spiritual state in 1924, the year she was asked to lead her first retreat at Pleshey.

Evelyn's final confessional letter to the Baron further outlined these lows. She described her 'constant conflict' with feelings of 'claimfulness, bitterness, jealousy, uncharitableness' which 'swamp' her soul. She felt 'incapable' of 'death to self', for her 'bad' nature dominated. But she also relayed how God sometimes came to her in a 'golden silence & peace', when she 'melts & vanishes & doesn't count' for 'He alone remains'. But despite her ceaseless 'craving' for God and her self-abandonment, all she could manage was to 'stand at the foot of the ladder and show people the way up'.[126] The Baron gently replied that 'self-satisfaction' or even appearing in our own eyes as having a 'satisfactory' state of soul is not a genuine measure of 'solid spiritual advancement'. He wanted her to 'gently drop' her '*vivacious irritated or confusing attention*' to her 'spiritual misery' through a 'quiet turning' to God, Christ and the poor. He believed this would help her 'grow in peace and power'.[127] So the Baron's final message to Evelyn was self-forgetfulness and reducing work to lessen strain.

The Baron's passing: A turning point

The Baron died in January 1925. Williams divides Evelyn's life into two parts, before and after the Baron's death.[128] For fifteen years Evelyn wrote about mystics and mysticism. For the next fifteen years, she introduced ordinary laypeople to the realities experienced by the mystics through providing homely metaphors that people could identify with, avoiding inaccessible, technical language. She was now venturing away from mysticism towards publications about the spiritual life.

Losing the Baron was, in Evelyn's words, 'a bit hard', but she found him 'awfully strong and happy' and very much 'with' her to the end.[129] In 1925 the Baron's niece Gwendolen Greene gave Evelyn notes on her final talk with the Baron plus some photos.[130] Gwen also showed Evelyn her letters from the Baron, which Evelyn found 'extraordinarily deep and beautiful, full of his peculiar wisdom and supernaturalness'. After reading them, Evelyn felt she understood von Hügel and his doctrine more than ever before; a year later, Evelyn talked with Gwen about the Baron – 'a great refreshment'.[131] Her ongoing friendship with Gwen continued, and in 1935 they met on the anniversary of the Baron's death, and thereafter Evelyn always thought of All Saints' Day as the Baron's feast day.[132]

When Gwen's letters were published in 1926 as *Letters from Baron Friedrich von Hügel to a Niece*, they brought Evelyn an 'extraordinary sense of contact with the Baron's spirit' plus a deep impression of his 'power and intensity', his 'passion for God' and the 'depth of the riches' he bestowed on her.[133] Evelyn's 'Green Notebook' has no entries for the year of the Baron's death.

In her book *Man and the Supernatural* (1927), Evelyn tried to express some of what she had learned from the Baron. Dedicating the book to his memory, she felt as if von Hügel were 'leaning over her shoulder' as she wrote; any 'value' it possessed came from his teaching.[134] She outlined her philosophy of religion based on the contrast between the supernatural and natural reality, illustrated through the 'duality of full human experience' and humanity's 'implicit participation' in both eternity and clock time.[135] One reviewer of the book claimed that Evelyn shared the 'biased views' of von Hügel – 'an accusation' she was happy to 'bear!'[136]

Formation through other spiritual directors

Following the Baron's death, Evelyn had two years without a spiritual director. At Easter in 1926 she recorded in her 'Flowered Notebook': 'fifteen months without direction' accompanied by much 'spiritual flatness' – 'loss of a director' is a 'very real grief', which leaves 'a blank behind'.[137] In late 1926 Evelyn asked Walter Howard Frere, the Anglican bishop of Truro, to be her spiritual director. He directed her until 1932. Interested primarily in the factual and in devout living, and not in the mystical, Frere was a complete contrast to both Evelyn and the Baron.[138] In eager anticipation, Evelyn copied her first letter to Frere in her 'Flowered Notebook', but surprisingly, she never transcribed any of his responding advice, as was her usual practice.

Letters from Frere that survived are warm but brief. He seemed to mull over Evelyn's letters for several weeks before providing his short reply. In one instance, he told her to ask for God's healing, encouraging her to 'welcome whatever pain is involved in ironing out the mischief', and not to bother about the symptoms, for God will 'do it in His own way'.[139] His response to her confession about her 'self-will and love of power' in direction work was calm: in working for others she would 'lose' herself and learn to consider her state 'irrelevant'. Rather than ponder her 'faults' or 'hover' over her 'sins', she was to be like St Paul – 'boldly . . . reach forward'.[140] Evelyn probably appreciated Frere's 'common sense, actuality and spirituality', which was recognized by some as similar to St Francis de Sales', but directees often found it difficult to get 'definite advice or opinions' from Frere, whose approach was 'diffident and tentative'.[141] Perhaps the most valuable aspect of Frere's spiritual direction was his introduction of Evelyn to the Russian Orthodox Church through meetings of the Fellowship of St Alban and St Sergius.[142] Despite this, during the final couple of years with Frere as director, Evelyn spent hours 'apparently' in prayer when really 'raging in hell' – experiencing 'furious and miserable thoughts', feeling 'absolutely wicked and vile'.[143] It was time to find a new director.

During her years of direction under Frere, Evelyn copied down the advice of Father Talbot and Bede Frost, and wrote letters to Abbot Chapman, which indicated that she was looking elsewhere for spiritual nurture. She described Abbot Chapman as 'my Abbot' and a 'contemplative saint', and met him in 1929 at Downside Abbey when visiting von Hügel's grave. She enjoyed Chapman's 'good sense' and 'fun' in his recounting of dealings with nuns who 'thought they had visions'.[144] Chapman gave Evelyn advice about activity and passivity in prayer and also discussed suffering as God's 'medicine', emphasizing the importance of 'acceptance'. He also encouraged Evelyn to live in the centre of a 'very frail life-boat in a strong sea', reassuring her that, as long as she was in the boat and not in the sea, all was well.[145] After his death in 1933, Chapman's *Spiritual Letters* were published and Evelyn repeatedly recommended them; she viewed him as a 'safe guide' who knew more about prayer than anyone else she had met.[146]

Evelyn also sought spiritual advice from Father Talbot, copying his counsel in her 'Flowered Notebook' (1929–30). Talbot told her to lead no more than six retreats a year to avoid 'overstrain'. He also encouraged her to concentrate on the 'good and loveable' in those who upset her, to offer her psychological suffering to God and to patiently bear her feelings of 'wickedness' – offering them to God and meeting 'panic' with a prayer of 'confidence'.[147] Evelyn also attended 'refreshing' retreats led by Talbot, sending 'helpful' notes from his talks to spiritual directees and encouraging them to seek him out.[148] Evelyn particularly appreciated that Talbot had been 'influenced' by the Baron's 'deep – deep wisdom and goodness'.[149] Her 'Flowered Notebook' also contained Evelyn's notes from a discussion with Father Bede in the late 1920s. He suggested Evelyn view her 'tumults' as 'purifying', 'accept' them 'peacefully' and align her will with God's. He also encouraged 'detachment' from her 'inordinate affection' for people.[150]

Father Reginald Somerset Ward, Evelyn's next main spiritual director, was with her till her death. After their first meeting in December 1932, Evelyn described him as the 'most remarkable soul-specialist' she had met since the Baron, recognizing their methods of direction and point of view as being '*very* close'.[151] Ward was in the rare position of being a full-time spiritual adviser for the Church of England. He was well suited to Evelyn given their shared belief in prayerful self-forgetfulness, his gift of spiritual discernment and his practice of providing 'strong' direction. He tended to see directees three times a year for a half-hour conversation when 'on tour', or a longer session if at home.[152] Evelyn saw him in Oxford and London and at his home in Farncombe; and when she was unwell later in life, Ward visited Evelyn at Hampstead.[153] Evelyn arrived feeling troubled on her first visit, as some Catholic friends had tried to convert her, saying her work for souls was wasted and harmful if she wasn't a Catholic.[154] Ward was able to reassure Evelyn and 'clear' her mind, and then he followed it with a 'rousing and fatherly' talk about the perils of overstrain.[155]

Ward believed that one pound of spiritual direction was composed of 'eight ounces of prayer, three ounces of theology, three ounces of common sense and two ounces of psychology'.[156] Having experienced mystical prayer, he converted the top room of his home into a chapel, with carvings of Richard Rolle, Julian of Norwich, St Teresa and St John of the Cross.[157] His method is outlined in his *A Guide for Spiritual Directors* (1957).

No letters between Ward and Evelyn have survived. The only evidence of Ward's spiritual formation of Evelyn are notes in her 'Flowered Notebook'. Her 1933 Easter confession to Ward reveals her fear of what 'total transformation' might cost, trying to 'dodge pain' from a lack of trust. Evelyn doubted whether she believed all she taught, giving the 'impression' she was far beyond what she lived by or even saw, then felt like an 'utter sham'. She recognized a 'deep gap' between action and prayer, for her prayers were 'fluctuating, distracted' and 'self-regarding'.[158] Evelyn harboured 'critical and unkind thoughts', together with 'explosions of irritation and hostile feelings' towards others and 'exasperation' towards anyone making 'demands' on her. She discerned a 'horrible streak' of 'hardness' and 'bitterness', as well as of being governed by her 'preference' for friends rather than by their 'needs'. She was also not interested in Hubert's affairs and found it difficult to love her father.[159] Ward's response was to instruct her to centre her effort on Christ's 'gentleness'. He wanted her to be Jesus' 'apprentice' in the 'art of living and dealing with people' and to imitate his (Jesus') actions. Evelyn was encouraged to plan and execute each week an act towards someone in this Christ-like 'spirit of gentleness', to help drive out her hardness, sharpness, criticism and uncharitable thoughts. She was not to increase her prayer, not to be excessive in self-examination and participate only in three-yearly confessions. Evelyn was to reduce tension and work, remembering that she was 'simply a channel for Christ's action', and in herself a 'humble and sinful soul' learning from Christ.[160] In May 1933 Evelyn described a 'bit of basting' from Ward and feeling 'better after that!' while on another occasion she described him being 'rather stern & stuffy' with her.[161]

Ward stated that a goal of spiritual direction is to discern the root fear that's weakening trust. By September 1933 he had diagnosed Evelyn's 'root trouble': 'possessiveness, deeply and suddenly injured and unable to adapt itself', resulting in a 'severe neurosis' which he saw as a 'deep scar' right across her soul. He believed it was aggravated by 'chronic overstrain' and suggested she 'avoid touching or rousing the wound' as it was 'still too tender to bear'. She was simply to 'accept' that bouts of suffering would arise and try to mortify 'possessiveness and claimfulness' in 'small things', relax her 'grip and clutch', and 'avoid all strain'.[162] In early 1934 Ward told Evelyn to remember that 'desire' in prayer was more important than 'satisfaction' and that her distracted condition arose from 'strain'. He reassured her that the 'whole of God's undivided love is poured out' on her soul and was the '*cause*' of her 'personality' and her 'power of response'. He encouraged her to think more of this than of her love for God and to open her soul to it.[163]

After a meeting with Ward in June that year, Evelyn noted she needed to be 'honest' with God and not 'blame' herself for what she couldn't help, such as 'distractions, temptations and uncharitable thoughts'. She should deal with distractions '*at once*' through taking a book, using the collect or writing down aspirations.[164] Ward now recommended confession only once a year, since it encouraged her 'subjectivism'. He wanted Evelyn to discriminate between 'temptation' and 'sin', encouraging her to stop struggling to be what she thought she'd 'like to be' but simply to 'yield' herself to God. Her prayer was to be something 'offered' to God, no matter how distracted, and she was to give 'affectionate attention' to her father and be 'actively sympathetic' to Hubert's interests. She was also to decide on the amount of 'rest and care' she required and to make it her 'duty' to achieve it.[165] Like von Hügel, Ward recommended 'hobbies' to balance work, for he believed that 'Overwork among conscientious souls is a far more real and frequent sin than laziness'.[166] As well as warning against the 'sin of overwork', he accentuated the importance of humour and that the life of prayer required what the Baron described as a 'circumambient air of leisure', thus he recommended Sabbath keeping and holidays.[167]

In 1936 Evelyn recorded her notes in preparation for a meeting with Ward. She was feeling 'reluctant' to give retreats and wondered if she had 'lost interest' or was simply aware of the 'effort'. She wanted to ask about a rule, communion and a quiet day each month, feeling that her life needed 'more careful organising' and she confessed her 'faults, nerves, irritability' and 'personal relations'.[168] Evelyn seemed content with Ward as her director. However, Armstrong believed that von Hügel was the one to 'transcend' all of Evelyn's other spiritual directors with his 'width and depth' of learning, 'sympathy and simplicity'.[169]

Two nuns were also important sources of spiritual nurture and support for Evelyn. In the autumn of 1925 Evelyn visited Sorella Maria di Campello – whom she called 'my Italian Saint' – at the ecumenical community of Bose in northern Italy.[170] She thought it 'wonderful' that Maria was 'extraordinarily like the Baron' in 'outlook', agreeing in 'all the deep things' of the spiritual life.[171] Sorella Maria was a significant confidante who enabled Evelyn to express her 'spiritual troubles'. Her short, telling replies provided comfort and sustenance.[172]

Evelyn also received spiritual nurture from Sr Mary of St John, a Carmelite nun living at a convent in Exmouth. Evelyn initially visited her in 1931, after which they corresponded until Evelyn's death, but only Sr Mary's letters have survived. Sr Mary referred to Evelyn as 'my dearest step-daughter' and repeatedly wrote of her 'desire' to see her.[173] Evelyn had described her 'devils and depressions' and 'uproar and unrest' when plunged into a whirl of activities, so Sr Mary was pleased to hear of Evelyn's 'definite stand' against public engagements, believing that such separation freed her soul.[174] Evelyn mentioned being 'used by God' but Sr Mary replied she was emphasizing that too much, arguing that it was a 'great thing not to make oneself too important to others or to think one is!'[175] In 1939 Evelyn described feeling 'distracted, dry and prayerless' but Sr Mary reassured her, encouraging her to 'sacrifice' reading war news so she could gain 'greater touch' with God.[176]

Formation through engagement in ecumenism

Like the Baron, Evelyn was an ecumenist, taking seriously the institutional practices of all branches of the Church. The Abbé Huvelin's influence had filtered through to her – Christianity's most profound enemy was anything making it 'narrow'.[177] Evelyn described herself as a 'scamp . . . unable to crystallize into the official shape'; the cat of 'any other Colour' in a cat show, illustrated her unique position.[178] Her 'particular call' was to the interior problems of individuals of 'all sorts and all opinions', to which end she used the general label of 'the Church' so that she didn't reduce her area of operation.[179] For Evelyn, the Church always meant the one undivided Church and, like von Hügel, she was the friend of every true Christian, no matter what branch they belonged to. As early as 1924, she described a meeting of the 'Christian Citizen Conference' as a 'triumph for the Spirit of Christ', as Anglicans, Roman Catholics and Nonconformists sat 'happily together' treating each other's beliefs with 'reverence'.[180] She felt 'in sympathy' with Christians of 'every sort – except when they start hating one another'.[181] She focused on the 'Church Invisible', seeing something 'entrancing' about the 'supernatural society – so wide and generous' wherein all Christians are one in Christ.[182]

Evelyn remained an Anglican her entire life but often worshipped in Catholic churches. She recognized Catholic books as the 'spiritual treasure of the Church Universal' and felt a 'great call' to help the 'renewal' of 'sane Catholicism' in England, viewing Anglicanism as part of a greater whole – 'a respectable suburb in the city of God'.[183] She didn't tolerate 'exclusiveness' in religion and believed we're all 'too narrow for God!' She clung to St Paul, finding his teaching relevant to everyone who 'cares for Christ', whether Catholic or Protestant.[184] Though she recognized 'superior food' in Roman Catholicism, she stated: 'our Lord has put me *here*, keeps on giving me more and more jobs to do for souls here, and has never given me orders to move.' She recalled the Baron's advice of never moving on account of your own 'religious preferences' but only if 'decisively called' by God.[185] Evelyn also recognized a desperate need in the Church of England for people who could help others in prayer, despite there being a great deal to 'put up with' and the diet 'often none too good'.[186] Her denominational allegiance came from her vocational calling, though Menzies remembered Evelyn wearing her Anglicanism with 'a difference'.[187]

In her later years, Evelyn's worship extended to Orthodox churches. She attended her first Orthodox fellowship conference in 1935, subsequently joining the Fellowship of St Alban and St Sergius. In 1938 she described Orthodox services as 'quite unimaginably lovely'; the combination of 'symbolic richness' and 'inner simplicity' resonated with her.[188] She appreciated how the Orthodox Church discovers the inward through the outward, 'weaving' together things of 'spirit and of sense'; as early as 1926 Evelyn recognized that mysticism based only on Catholic and Protestant mystics was 'lop-sided' and 'incomplete'.[189]

Evelyn's book *Worship*, published in 1936, was an attempt to define the human response to the eternal. She surveyed the unique elements of worship in Catholicism, Judaism, Eastern Orthodoxy and Anglicanism and in the Reformed and Free churches. She wanted to show them as 'chapels of various types' but as 'one Cathedral of the Spirit', leading human souls by 'different ways' to 'adoration'.[190]

It became the 'Religious Book of the Month' in the United States in 1937. Her book was a success partly because she knew the subject from the 'inside'.[191] A massive shift had occurred between Evelyn's major works – *Mysticism* and *Worship* – the latter being much more incarnational, sacramental and institutional.

Prayer was viewed by Evelyn as the essential ingredient of ecumenical unity. In 1920 she was involved in the Confraternity of the *Spiritual Entente*, serving as secretary and writing a leaflet explaining its aims.[192] This fellowship, founded by Sorella Maria, was a dispersed ecumenical movement of Christians praying for church unity, though retaining their own church affiliation. Its only rule was to refrain from criticizing other forms of Christianity, to find Christ in every Christian's soul and to 'diffuse' this 'spirit', allowing it to secretly spread like leaven. Each person acted as a 'link' in an 'invisible chain' of spiritual understanding.[193] Later in 1938, Evelyn was one of the original participants in a prayer movement for church reunion before the Feast of the Transfiguration.

Evelyn's letters to Maisie Spens similarly reveal her prayer focus on ecumenism. Spens was part of Abbé Couturier's Reunion Movement, emphasizing the union of Christians through prayer. Rather than enter into theological arguments and 'ecclesiastical controversies', Evelyn believed that a widespread group of praying souls was essential for church unity: the Church would win the world for Christ only through 'living spirits steeped in prayer'.[194] She believed that the reunion of the churches would be the 'flower of a seed sown long before in the fields of the Spirit and cherished in secret by a few'.[195] Thus she encouraged her retreatants: 'never break our brotherhood with those who come longer journeys by other paths, led by a different star.'[196]

Formation through pacifism

During the Second World War Evelyn became an ardent pacifist. She joined the Anglican Pacifist Fellowship and the Peace Pledge Union and wrote for the Fellowship of Reconciliation. Evelyn argued that war is 'not Christian' as it's in 'direct conflict' with brotherly love.[197] She believed the Church would lose its 'supernatural call' if it were involved in war, as evil is not fought with evil, but is 'vanquished' only through '*love*'.[198] Hitler could be met with 'war' or 'the Cross', Evelyn declared, but only a small number are 'ready for the Cross' in the 'full sense of loving': 'this alone is full Christianity.'[199]

As in ecumenism, prayer was central to 'Christian love in action', according to Evelyn, as the origins lie with 'demonic powers'. Thus Evelyn argued for the need to fight in the invisible world by praying for dictators' hearts; thus she encouraged her prayer group to engage in 'spiritual war-work', prayer.[200] The praying pacifist has 'crossed over' to God's side and 'stands by the Cross' – the supreme expression of love and trusting the unseen – with '*eyes cleansed by prayer*' we see life in this 'supernatural' way.[201]

In this way, the true pacifist was a 'redeemer', engaged in a 'supernatural vocation', and the Church should 'spread' this Spirit of Christ by defeating evil through love.[202] It is through the power of prayer that those 'hidden, spiritual forces' intervene. This was Evelyn's 'doctrine of non-resistance' – 'universal charity'.[203] And this loving 'non-resistance' was organic, so Evelyn encouraged 'cells of tranquillity' in a world at war, believing that the peace would 'radiate' through 'slowly spreading circles', making a 'true' contribution.[204]

Formation through suffering ill health

As early as 1927, Evelyn was fragile looking but with 'wonderfully alive' eyes.[205] In 1930 she reflected that she would likely have 'indifferent' health for the rest of her life and must face this reality 'quietly and gratefully', avoid dwelling on her physical state as the centre of the picture and accept the 'monotony' and 'humbling details' of illness with 'JOY'.[206] Evelyn's fragile physical health was partly the result of giving so much of her soul, mind and body to others.[207]

Just before the Second World War, the Stuart Moores moved in with the Vernons on the Sussex Downs. Evelyn had chronic asthma, and by 1939 the younger Marjorie Vernon was caring for her, as she and Hubert were (in Evelyn's words), 'physical crocks'.[208] Evelyn had met Marjorie earlier, as she had wanted to talk about her religious difficulties. On their first meeting they had 'clicked', discussing everything but religion.[209] Having to depend on others for help was not easy, yet Evelyn recognized it as a 'marvellous discipline', introducing her to a 'fresh' set of 'tests' and 'opportunities', as well as the discovery of devoted kindness.[210] During this period, Evelyn was asked to teach religion to village children. When she asked them 'Why do we praise God?' she was rather delighted when a child replied, 'To cheer Him up!'[211]

In 1938 Evelyn was made a doctor of divinity by Aberdeen University but was too unwell to receive the honour in person. She found it 'quite startling' and a 'bit comic', and couldn't help 'wishing' it had been from the University of St Andrews, the Baron's 'glory hole' for his first honorary doctorate, his second DD having been awarded by the University of Oxford.[212]

Four weeks before her death, while bedridden with pain, Evelyn 'sent messages' asking for prayers for the 'union' of Christian churches. She reached a 'climax' when the 'distress seemed to be spiritual', then her face's relief revealed 'something . . . accomplished'.[213]

Evelyn died on 15 June 1941 from a thrombosis. Her will declared her funeral be conducted in a 'simple' manner, without flowers, mourning or 'lugubrious' hymns.[214] Her treasured possessions were to be given to special friends. Lucy Menzies was bequeathed Evelyn's Russian crucifix, which she had worn when conducting retreats, her Trinity icon, Eternity embroidery and devotional books. Her autographed copy of *Eternal Life* and the Baron's letters were entrusted to Marjorie Vernon.[215] She also bequeathed money to the Royal Society for the Protection of Birds.

Since 2000 the Church of England has commemorated Evelyn liturgically on 15 June. This is also Evelyn's feast day in the liturgical calendar for the Episcopal Church in the United States, where she is particularly revered by the active Evelyn Underhill Association, which holds an annual quiet day and publishes a biennial newsletter. Evelyn authored or edited thirty-nine books and about 350 articles and reviews. However, she sometimes felt that her words were 'probably nonsense'.[216] Archbishop Ramsay claims that during the 1920s and 1930s, Evelyn did more than anyone to help people in the Church of England 'grasp' the 'priority of prayer' and the 'place' of the 'contemplative element' within it.[217]

Having highlighted some of Evelyn's narrative, we now turn to examine the Baron's spiritual formation of Evelyn, the person of whom she wrote 'I owe . . . my whole spiritual life'.

3

The Baron's spiritual formation of Evelyn Underhill

His supreme interest . . . lay in souls and their growth – in arousing the deepest reality of man to the overwhelming Reality . . . he recognized, and valued, many diverse means as serving this great end.[1]

I owe him my whole spiritual life . . . that immense and transforming help . . .[2]

These words from Evelyn Underhill in 1931 reveal that she was unequivocal that the Baron had significantly transformed her spiritual life. She added that there would have been 'much more' transformation if she had been 'more courageous and stern' with herself and 'followed his directions more thoroughly'.[3] Evelyn 'drank deeply' of von Hügel's spirit, describing him as her 'final court of appeal' on all questions concerning the inner life.[4]

Three elements of religion

Von Hügel's three 'elements of religion', as outlined in his magnum opus, *The Mystical Element of Religion*, provided an explicit organizing principle for his life and his spiritual direction of Evelyn. The Baron argued that *all* three elements – the 'Intellectual element' (rational and theological), the 'Mystical element' (experiential and devotional) and the 'Institutional element' (including church involvement, the sacraments, community and tradition) – are required for a full and balanced Christian life. To omit one would diminish our response to God. He noted our tendency to 'specialize' in one element over the others, for the three elements each tend to continually 'tempt' the soul to 'retain only it'.[5] Evelyn recognized the three elements as the Baron's 'governing intuition' in the 'many-levelled richness and complexity' of our lives, as well as the 'dangerous silliness of simplification' when it is applied to the mystery of our inner life.[6]

Balancing the elements of religion involved an awareness, even a cultivation, of the tension or friction between them. Von Hügel drew 'spiritual sustenance' through experiencing these 'costing' tensions, bracing himself for this 'growth through tension'.[7] This friction between the elements aiding spiritual growth was vividly conveyed through two images. The first image of 'confluentia' is when a body of water forms when two or more rivers flow together, such as the joining of the Rosel and Rhine rivers in Switzerland. The merging of the energy of the rivers, with all their turbulence and power, is akin to the bracing of the soul when it holds the different elements together in tension. The second image is that of a frog eating crickets, which die cross-wise in its abdomen. The frog pats its stomach so that the food conforms to its stomach shape. This contrasting image is a slow process, involving 'considerable friction generated and overcome', as the raw material becomes conformed to the container in which it finds itself.[8] These two images offer contrasting characterizations of the friction between the elements that the Baron felt to be essential for souls to 'grow and become'.[9] Evelyn recalled this notion of friction as one of the Baron's 'fundamental' convictions regarding our spiritual lives.[10]

Evelyn came to von Hügel as an intellectual who had already published several books, having had mystical experiences but not much sustained involvement in the Church. He diagnosed her as having an excess of the intellectual element and a spirituality disconnected from the historical Christ and the Church, and thought she therefore needed to be brought into balance and tension with the institutional element, particularly the historical and Christocentric.

The institutional element

The image von Hügel often used to describe the Church's role in spiritual formation was of trees being slowly shaped by sea breezes. He spoke of a childhood memory in Brussels where the trees stood 'permanently fixed in every kind of unnatural, fleeing or defiant, attitude and angle'.[11] Those trees remained for him a vivid image of the crucial, inexorable force of the Church on masses of humans, and as being required in Evelyn's spiritual formation.

Encouragement to church involvement

The Baron encouraged Evelyn into regular church involvement, acutely aware of how he'd been 'formed' by the Church himself, how his whole life and practice had been 'inspired' by the Church's teaching and doctrine – his soul 'fed' by the church's 'soul'.[12] He longed for Evelyn to see the 'huge, irreplaceable good' we all 'owe' to the Church, the basis of all 'real sanctity' and the means by which we become 'deep' and 'humble'.[13]

However, despite being aware of his debt to the Church and its profound importance, he was also acutely aware that church involvement carries great 'cost', requiring 'heroism'.[14] For, though the Church provides 'insights and aids', it also has 'deadlocks' and 'obstacles'.[15] Von Hügel went so far as to describe institutional Christianity as his 'hair-shirt' and 'deepest pain'; yet he viewed 'costingness' and 'tension' as two 'great elements of growth', and pain as the 'greatest teacher', 'discipline', 'training' and 'food'.[16]

In his view, Evelyn needed to develop an institutional, sacramental religion to counter her pure mysticism. Von Hügel encouraged her to attend church of some kind each Sunday, 'preferably' Holy Communion and one weekday mass at the Carmelites, though he was careful to protect her from 'over-burdening'.[17] Later, he suggested a 'rule' of communion twice a week, with occasional attendance three or four times a week.[18] However, given Evelyn's temperament, he feared her 'overdoing' institutionalism, so suggested she fix on a 'certain minimum, a nucleus' of church practice, and to be careful not to add to it when in consolation or detract from it when in desolation.[19]

Over a few years, Evelyn went from viewing the Church as being like a post office, with irritating, narrow-minded officials behind the counter, to 'feel[ing] the regular, steady, docile practice of corporate worship' as being of the 'utmost importance' for 'building up' her spiritual life. She argued that no amount of solitary prayer or reading makes up for 'humble immersion' in the 'life and worship' of the Church.[20] Evelyn became a member of St Paul's, Vicarage Gate, and also attended the local Carmelite church. She was also attentive to the 'Church Invisible', which the Baron recognized as one of the 'great centralities' of religion – 'Look up! Look up! what a glorious, touching company'.[21]

The communal aspect of Church as the great 'interconnection of souls' was also emphasized by von Hügel.[22] Underlying this image was his conviction that all reality is a 'multiplicity in unity, an interchange and mutual help and stimulation of complimentary gifts and powers'.[23] Thus as individuals we are 'constituted' into persons, never simply in 'isolation' but 'always within, and for, and in friction with, complexes'.[24] We grow with and through others, never simply within and through ourselves, and thus 'moulding' into 'persons' comes through our willing service of family and Church.[25] The Baron believed that the Church 'conceives humanity' as individuals give their 'gold dust' as to a 'great piece of gold', for individuals come to 'much more development' as part of that 'larger whole', thus Jesus always 'banded people together'.[26] Evelyn came to recognize the significance of the soul's relation to others through hearing von Hügel criticize people like George Fox, who 'cut themselves off' from others in the service of religion.[27] The Baron also critiqued the 'grave omissions' of Plotinus' 'unsocial conception' of the 'alone with the Alone', for religion is 'never' entirely 'individual' but always 'social and institutional'.[28]

Another benefit of Church community is encouragement during times of dryness and spiritual desolation. Von Hügel wrote that in 'periods of obscurity' we live in the faith of other believers, observing their vivid, 'seeing love'.[29] A related benefit is receiving spiritual nurture from more mature Christians in the community: the 'older, more experienced soul' can 'cheer us on', reminding us that faithfully living through 'vicissitudes' can help us grow 'strong' and 'deep' in God.[30]

Such learning in community is essential, von Hügel argued, for we shall never learn much about religion unless more mature souls 'touched' by God 'help us on our way'.[31] In 1923, when Evelyn was paralysed by doubts about whether her experiences were imaginary self-suggestion, the Baron consolingly reassured her of their authenticity, but warned her against 'craving . . . certainty', for such experiences are not articles of faith like God and Christ.[32]

Living in two worlds – spirit and sense

Another key aspect of the institutional element is the duality of our human existence as 'inseparably mixed, spirit *and sense*, creature[s]'.[33] Von Hügel argued:

> You see how the sensible always conveys the spiritual: the invisible in the visible. Christ everywhere makes use of the sensible to convey the spiritual, never the spirit alone. Man is spirit and body; he has arms and legs, he is not spirit alone . . . The spirit is stimulated through the senses . . . Christ never left them out: the woman who touched him, the clay on the eyes. He always and everywhere makes use of the sensible. Thus the bread and the wine.[34]

This interplay between the sensual and the spiritual is because we live in 'two worlds' and the essence of religion is the supernatural life, the other world, the 'otherness of God, different from, but penetrating' this life.[35] Therefore the primary end and function of the Church is 'awakening souls' and developing an 'other-worldly' sense through holding before congregants 'embodiments' of the life beyond the grave.[36] Von Hügel saw the temporal as a dwelling place for the eternal, with no separation between natural and supernatural, for the two are 'woven so closely together' that they are one.[37] He emphasized to Evelyn this 'interweaving' which she later recalled as the Baron's 'doubleness', his capacity for moving between 'natural and supernatural levels', which ran right through his life and teaching.[38] As Armstrong argued, von Hügel fed Evelyn with this 'nourishment' which led to a 'complete reorientation' of her understanding and a new 'foundation', in a way that 'perhaps no one else could have done'.[39]

Von Hügel insisted on the 'incurably amphibious' character of humans – 'conditioned by the senses', yet 'craving the super-sensual'.[40] This dual reality was reflected in a twofold movement of alternating between engaging in the concrete, physical world and in the abstract, spiritual reality. He argued that the soul can live only by this 'double process' of 'occupation with the concrete' and 'abstraction' from it; without the latter it becomes 'empty and hazy', but without the former it grows 'earthly and heavy'.[41] The Baron held that both the 'world-fleeing' movement essential to all deep religion and the 'friction' of the 'world-seeking' element are essential to faith, believing this 'two-fold movement'– this ebb and flow from and to the world – as 'cryingly wanted'.[42] Steere viewed this 'flowing out' of prayer into the full life in the world and the use of the 'frictional' material from the world to drive us more deeply into prayer as von Hügel's 'distinctive' contribution.[43]

The Baron was highly sensitive to any teaching 'despising' matter or declaring the Spirit alone to be 'real'.[44] Thus he criticized Friedrich Heiler's book *Prayer* (1921) for its 'exclusion' of the 'sensual'.[45] He also critiqued Luther's doctrine that forbade anything 'sensual' for fear of 'stimulating the spiritual', asking whether the 'sensual [was] a blind alley'. Doesn't it come from God and wasn't it 'intended for the spiritual' as a 'bridge to the spiritual'? Why should our body and senses remain 'outside' when we pray?[46] The origin of the 'anti-sacramental passion' of many Protestants was seen by von Hügel to have 'understandable' causes such as a terror of priestly domination, but to 'cut the knots' doesn't resolve the difficulty; 'sensible things' are 'joint-awakeners' in the spiritual life that sanctify, as shown in the lives of Jesus and St Paul.[47] Thus, for von Hügel, the sensual was a bridge to the spiritual, particularly via 'symbols and sacraments' – contacts between spirit and matter.[48]

Sacraments

The senses – particularly through the sacraments – awaken the soul. Von Hügel told Evelyn that we never begin or keep up, in the long run, our 'apprehension' of spiritual things except through the 'stimulation' of the senses; awareness is always a 'doubly dual consciousness' of 'sensible and mental', and thus we require 'stimulations' to develop an understanding of God's 'personalness through things' – the sacraments.[49]

Von Hügel described the sacraments as a 'great incarnational doctrine' in keeping with the 'mysterious double-sidedness' – the matter and spirit of our humanity.[50] Involvement in the sacraments is not just a reflection of love, but actually *produces* love and growth, as he described vividly: 'I kiss my child not only because I love it; I kiss it also in order to love it.' He recognized this as a 'sheer fact traceable throughout our many-sided life', that we 'often grow, mentally and spiritually, almost solely by the stimulation of our senses'.[51] He therefore emphasized the 'profound importance' that Evelyn frequently engage in the sacraments, for he had practised and tested them for over fifty years and found them the 'greatest use'.[52]

The Eucharist

This view of the sacraments obviously comes into particular focus in the Eucharist. Von Hügel believed that taking communion should be the 'very centre' of Evelyn's devotional life for it is the 'basis of all real sanctity' and 'fruit bearing', having built up saints.[53] In 1921 Evelyn was told that, if she could attend only one church service a week, it should preferably be Holy Communion. Similarly, in 1922 she was encouraged to concentrate on attending Holy Communion.[54] In 1923 the Baron recommended that Evelyn attend a minimum of two communions a week when spiritually dry, and to go 'occasionally' three or four times a week.[55] He argued that we gain two 'contradictory outlooks' on life according to whether we partake in the Eucharist or not, so Evelyn indicated that she would 'never sacrifice' communion unless it was impossible, such as when yachting.[56]

The effect of the Eucharist on von Hügel was profound: 'afterwards I feel expanded – I breathe deeply in a great deliverance.'[57] Von Hügel spoke repeatedly about the real presence of Christ in the Eucharist and in his visit to the Blessed Sacrament, stating he was as 'certain' of the real presence of Christ in the Eucharist as he was of anything.[58] Gwen Greene recalled von Hügel saying, 'Christ ever reincarnates Himself', referring to the mystical presence of Christ in the Eucharist. The Baron took his communion for Evelyn when she was experiencing difficulty.[59]

The body

As well as emphasizing human beings as 'mixed' creatures, both 'spirit and body' – 'physico-spiritual' organisms – von Hügel emphasized the 'ceaseless interdependence' of body and soul.[60] He wrote, 'God is the God of the body as He is of the soul', thus we need to cultivate 'reverence' for the body to stay 'sane' and 'balanced'.[61]

Evelyn had experienced the 'parallels' between nervous states and spiritual sensitiveness, finding her 'nerves and soul . . . hopelessly mixed up'; thinking she was 'out of grace', she'd discover it was simply 'mental fatigue'.[62] She asked von Hügel to help her run her devotional life when in 'nervous exhaustion', even requesting a 'modern equivalent' of a 'hairshirt' to remind her to escape pure mysticism and her anti-institutional bias.[63] Von Hügel was not interested in subjecting her body to excessive asceticism, but rather in her holding sensuality and spirituality together. He was acutely aware that the incarnational side of religion must never be 'forgotten' but, rather, assigned a 'definite place' in our spiritual lives, so he endeavoured to help Evelyn become 'continuously alive' to the action of the body, senses, sensible objects and the physical environment in relation to her spiritual life.[64]

Von Hügel outlined this interplay of body and soul when he wrote that God is an 'immense *concretion*, not an abstraction', and that he made our body and senses so that we can '*incarnate*' the '*incarnate* God'. This involves not simply expressing 'spirit in and through matter' but also awakening and causing to grow through the friction from 'contacts' between 'my spirit from, and to, matter'. Thus the spirit is not 'floating' or 'drifting' above the body or institutions such as the family, but 'penetrating into' them and 'retiring out' from them.[65]

The Baron believed that we gain a 'full sense' of God through contact with matter. He went so far as to argue that we won't attain a 'thoroughly wholesome, deeply spiritual religion' unless we give it 'a body' – 'contacts with the visible', for religion requires attention to 'visible and audible institutional and social acts and rites', without which we cannot 'fully capture and maintain a deep, wholesome . . . spirituality'.[66] Further, he argued, Christianity 'does not ignore or neglect', but 'enters into and sanctifies', the body.[67] He balanced the doctrine of God as Spirit with the Word made flesh, arguing that these two things together constitute Christianity's force, whereas 'contempt for, or absence' of the 'practice' of the 'visible' or 'audible' produces 'spiritual emptiness, restlessness and inflation'.[68]

In practical terms, this leads to a need to manage our thinking and feeling by finding ways to relax and exercise the body. Gwen

Greene summed it up as the 'balance' in Christianity between the 'twin life' that feeds body and spirit, enclosing our whole self.[69] After Evelyn's mother's death and her inheritance, von Hügel recommended that Evelyn drop her writing output to two-thirds, to enable more rest, which he believed, would help her soul 'advance'.[70]

Alongside this incarnational focus, von Hügel emphasized the importance of the historic and Christocentric in the institutional element of religion.

History and Christ

Von Hügel repeatedly argued that history is the 'crux' of institutional religion.[71] By this he meant that only in and through 'concrete happenings in time and space' do we 'awaken' to God, for all genuine religion requires 'really *happened* Historical Facts and Persons', and Christianity's 'greatness' comes from this 'incarnational trend': God 'revealed' himself and 'touches' us through 'duration' and 'matter'.[72] In other words, only as God entered history in the past have we been provided with historical facts whereby God's action is seen, and only as he enters the present, revealing himself, are we awakened to God. The same twofold understanding of history is seen (in reverse order) in the Baron's essay on Christ: our souls are only 'awakened to the presence of spiritual realities when a contingent and historical stimulus from without excites them', hence the incarnation.[73]

Von Hügel stated that he 'couldn't live without' a religion 'full of history'.[74] In his spiritual direction, this idea of historicity was most marked in his focus on the historical Christ. Evelyn came to von Hügel with no relationship with Jesus, and a largely Unitarian mindset. Addressing her neglect of the incarnational aspect of religion in the person of Jesus became central to von Hügel's direction. He encouraged Evelyn to 'feel the factualness, the happenedness [*sic*] of our Lord, of His Passion' and of the 'Holy Communion', and thereby 'feed and articulate' the Christocentric movement.[75]

He asked Evelyn to 'work gently but wholeheartedly' at getting this principle of 'Historical Happenings' to become one of the 'chief beams' of her 'spiritual edifice, part of the rock, known and willed at all times', for 'belief' in them is 'necessary'.[76]

Evelyn was glad the Baron had 'stirred' her up concerning the Christocentric, incarnational side of religion, for left to herself she would 'just go off on god alone'. But the Baron made her see 'it simply *won't do*' and leads to 'arrogance' plus missing some of Christianity's 'loveliest, deepest and most touching parts'.[77] He told Evelyn that God dwells in and manifests himself through 'Historical Happenings' such as the manger and the cross, and that this 'incarnational' understanding is the only 'completely creaturely' temper of mind leading to a religion 'sufficiently lowly, homely, humbling'.[78] Even more simply, von Hügel encouraged Evelyn to try 'at least *thinking* of Our Lord' at Holy Communion but Evelyn exclaimed, 'Christo-centric devotion . . . I can't do it'.[79] The Baron replied to her question about how to 'slip in' some Christocentric devotion by encouraging her to give 'special care' to the 'historical, incarnational current' which had been 'starved' to date. But if she couldn't pray to Jesus she should at least try to 'pray to God Unincarnate with thought and affections' towards Nazareth, Lake Galilee and Calvary where love was shown 'for God' and 'by God'.[80] Over time, Evelyn gradually shifted from her 'purely mystical and philosophic' beginnings to a more Catholic, incarnational spirituality, the 'two currents' becoming 'interwoven, with special care given to the sacramental'.[81]

By 1922 Evelyn was describing how the Baron had enabled her to 'bridge the gap' between theism and Christian devotion which had worried her for years; now she had her 'universe all in one piece again' with the 'transcendental and incarnational' currents 'woven together'. But she declared that the 'incarnational current' was still the 'weakest', though she persisted in meditating on the New Testament to 'strengthen' the strictly Christian side.[82]

A year later she was able to write to von Hügel:

The Christocentric side has become so much deeper and stronger – it nearly predominates. I never dreamed it was like this. It's just beginning now to dawn on me what the Sacramental Life really does involve: but it is only in flashes of a miraculous penetration I can realize this . . . I have never known before such deep and real happiness, such a sense of at last having got my real permanent life and being able to love without stint where I am meant to love. It is as if one were suddenly liberated and able to expand all round. Such joy that it sometimes almost hurts. All this, humanly speaking, I owe entirely to you.[83]

In 1927 she recorded her spiritual development in this moving testimony:

Until about five years ago I never had any personal experience of our Lord. I didn't know what it meant. I was a convinced Theocentric, and thought Christocentric language and practice sentimental and superstitious . . . when I went to the Baron he said I wasn't much better than a Unitarian. Somehow by his prayers or something, he compelled me to experience Christ. He never said anything more about it – but I know humanly speaking he did it. It took about four months – it was like watching the sun rise very slowly – and then suddenly one knew what it was . . . for the next two or three years, and especially lately, more and more my whole religious life and experience seem to centre with increasing vividness on our Lord – that sort of quasi involuntary prayer which springs up of itself at odd moments is always now directed to Him . . . The New Testament, which once I couldn't make much of, or meditate on, now seems full of things never noticed – all gets more and more alive and compellingly beautiful . . . Holy Communion which at first I did simply under obedience, gets more and more wonderful too.[84]

Despite this development, five years later, Evelyn was aware of being 'instinctively pulled' to the theocentric side, for her soul went 'naturally' in that direction when left to itself. She wrote, 'I come to Christ through God' and thus she found it difficult to show people how to come 'to God through Christ'.[85] Evelyn recalled how the Baron argued that a 'well-balanced' religion requires the 'theocentric *and* incarnational sides together', though she struggled with her sense of God swamping the Christocentric sense.[86] As a spiritual director, Evelyn stated that the saints taught that it's 'far better & safer' to contemplate God through the 'Humanity of Christ', than 'any other way'.[87]

In closing our discussion of the institutional element, we shall see how Evelyn absorbed some of the Baron's insights in her Preface to the twelfth edition of *Mysticism* in 1930. She wrote that if she were to rewrite the text she would have emphasized the 'twin doctrines' highlighted in the Baron's work: first, that mysticism is never the 'whole content' of religion but requires 'history, dogma and institutions'; and, second, that the 'antithesis' between the Church and the mystic is false as 'each requires the other'.[88] This summary reveals two key developments in Evelyn's spiritual formation through engaging in the institutional element. We now turn to examine von Hügel's encouragement of Evelyn in terms of the mystical element. Though all three elements 'grew' and were in 'constant interaction' in the Baron's life, the mystical element most attracted him, enabling him to flourish.[89]

The mystical element

The mystical element was the element von Hügel discussed most with his directees. However, as Evelyn recalled, the mystical element was not allowed to 'dominate the field' or become the 'one basis' of faith.[90] It needed to be balanced and kept honest by the other two elements. In fact, if mysticism became the 'whole' of religion, it was in 'dangerous error'.[91] The Baron thus emphasized the difference between 'Pure or Sheer or Exaggerated Mysticism' (akin to pantheism or spiritualism) and 'Mixed or Moderate Mysticism', which finds its 'completion, articulation and safety' in institutions and history.[92] Evelyn was encouraged away from her exclusive focus on contemplative prayer, her 'pure' mysticism, to this 'mixed' mysticism, where she balanced her prayer of quiet with corporate prayer and acts of service to others.

Spiritual disciplines

The Baron introduced Evelyn to spiritual disciplines that would help her grow spiritually and more fully experience the 'golden shower from above'.[93] The specific diet of practices was recommended according to her *attrait*, or type. The Baron had a profound reverence for the differences in souls, arguing that they are 'never dittos'. Being aware of these variations wakes us up so we can be more 'sensitive and perceptive' to directees.[94] Von Hügel was also careful to provide prayer advice that was appropriate to each person's particular 'stage' of development, warning against 'indigestible morsels' and once telling Evelyn, 'they may be food for other souls, and perhaps even for *yours*, in a later stage of its growth!'[95] These convictions were painfully learned when the Baron attempted to shape his own daughter Gertrud on the basis of his own *attrait*.

Adoration

Adoration is key to spiritual growth and the foundation for prayer, according to the Baron. He declared that the 'first and central act of religion is *adoration*, sense of God' – this is the very 'soul of religion'.[96] He went so far as to say that religion without adoration is like a 'triangle with one side left out', and thus he encouraged directees to the 'spontaneous habit' of small exclamations of adoration to God.[97] In Evelyn's subsequent spiritual direction of others, she adopted this repeated focus on adoration.

Prayer

The Baron suggested that Evelyn pray whatever kind of prayer suited her best, that is, what most strengthened her to love, work, suffer and be humbled. He encouraged her to have a 'prayerful disposition' penetrating her working hours, but at other times he gave her specific instructions regarding prayer: 'practise the mixed kind of prayer you describe and no formal meditation' for sixty or ninety minutes daily.[98]

But von Hügel emphasized flexibility and was careful not to overburden Evelyn: 'when you cannot get to the Carmelites', she was to give those fifteen minutes to 'some kind of prayer' at home.[99] Similarly, he encouraged her to have a definite time for daily '*deliberate prayer*', adding that it should not be long and should consist of whatever kind of prayer most strengthened her to love.[100] Being aware of the 'exhausting' nature of the prayer of quiet, he cautioned that it was 'wise' to do 'rather less' of this 'delightful' prayer than one felt 'drawn to'.[101]

In 1923 he suggested that Evelyn drop all 'voluntary self-occupation' during the day by gently turning to God in Christ. He viewed this as a suitable substitute for self-examination that would help her 'grow'. God would give her 'glimpses' of any 'imperfect dispositions' through this 'simple flight away from self to God and Christ', which he believed, would 'brace' her.[102]

Evelyn told the Baron that her prayer was still 'mixed' but was 'more passive: a sort of inarticulate communion, or aspirations, often merely one word, over and over'.[103] She described two prayer practices: twenty minutes of a 'warm inhibited darkness and blind joy' when she 'lives in Eternity', in addition to praying a few psalms each day, but she confessed that she struggled with intercession.[104] The Baron was satisfied with both forms of prayer, assuring her that intercessory prayer would come. Once again, he emphasized prayer as the background for all her activities, plus three to five minutes of examination of conscience each night before sleeping.[105] In 1923 he wrote that her 'present mixed consciousness and action', despite loss of prayer of quiet, showed a 'gain' in 'genuine' spirituality.[106]

Silence was emphasized by von Hügel as 'fundamental' in attaining the spiritual life.[107] He stressed that at 'no time is over-much talking compatible with spiritual growth', so Evelyn should learn 'interior silence': 'Don't chatter to yourself – you can't hear God if you do.'[108] And a prerequisite for silence is solitude, although the Baron added that if it were really required, we can trust God to provide it and, if he doesn't, simply carry on tranquilly without it.[109] Evelyn was also told to practise Brother Lawrence's secret of having a 'prayerful disposition' penetrate working hours.[110] Von Hügel encouraged Evelyn to a gentle 'feeding of the dim background' of her studies and composition with a sense that all she is doing is beyond her – aware of an 'awe-inspiring Over-againstness' – and responding with short 'aspirations' to God during breaks between her tasks.[111] Alongside this dim background, Evelyn summarized 'self-abandonment' as the 'crowning virtue' suggested by the Baron, with 'humbling and bracing' as the twin qualities to be looked for in prayer and spiritual reading.[112]

The mixed life

The life of prayer alone was always to be balanced with a life with and for others. Thus von Hügel encouraged his directees to love and help many souls but also reminded them – 'be alone . . . Then you will be near God!'[113] So Evelyn was told to balance her prayer with parental visits – 'humbly . . . increase their quality from your parents' standpoint' – hoping for a corresponding expansion in her love for them.[114] For von Hügel, spiritual growth comes from giving in caring relationships, hence his final words: 'Christianity has taught us to care . . . caring matters most.'[115]

Visiting the poor

These deliberate acts of service were not to be limited to family, however. Evelyn was encouraged to visit the poor, to help balance out what von Hügel saw as her excess of the intellectual element. Von Hügel suggested that Evelyn visit the poor two afternoons a week, striving to 'spread the spirit' derived from those two days over the other five, giving 'preference' to these bi-weekly visitations above 'everything else'.[116] Evelyn started visiting eight poor families two afternoons a week and judged von Hügel's 'prescription' a 'complete success'; she had been 'starving' for something of this kind and couldn't even describe the 'sense of expansion and liberation' she received.[117] Following each visit she felt an 'utter worm' as she compared her own secure life with their 'incessant struggles and anxieties' and the 'amazing courage' with which they bore them. She wrote that, however 'jangled' she felt when visiting them, she always returned 'mysteriously filled with peace and nearer God' – they gave her much more than she could ever give them.[118] Von Hügel believed that the poor have a 'humbling and spiritualising influence'; Evelyn recalled 'God, Christ and the Poor' as a 'trilogy' frequently found in the Baron's letters.[119]

Spiritual/devotional reading

Spiritual reading was another spiritual discipline von Hügel routinely recommended to his directees. His fifteen minutes of daily spiritual reading was described as one of the 'great sustenances' and 'sources of calm' of his life over decades.[120] This lingering, prayerful reading was described through vivid images, such as 'letting a very slowly dissolving lozenge melt imperceptibly in your mouth' or a 'caramel slowly dissolving'.[121] It is 'slow, ruminating', 'devotional' and prayerful, excluding all criticism, as the aim is to feed our soul with a sense of 'loving God'.[122] Directees were told to not exceed fifteen minutes or it would sink into 'ordinary' reading; it was to become as 'regular as washing'.[123]

The *effect* of such reading was frequently described; it would 'feed' the heart and 'fortify' the will, putting directees into 'contact' with God and the realities it suggests.[124] When suffering, these readings 'become alive' with Christ and they 'foster and feed' a sense of God's presence throughout the day, becoming 'background', 'support', 'light', 'balm and refreshment'.[125]

The Baron suggested many spiritual classics but Evelyn was able to disregard those of his recommendations that didn't resonate. He 'dosed' her with Fénelon at one time until she told him that a 'Perfect Gentleman giving judicious spiritual advice to Perfect Ladies was no good' for her, and thereafter his name was no longer mentioned![126]

As well as spiritual classics, Scripture was recommended, for it 'strengthened' the Baron's 'outlook' every 'day and hour'.[127] The 'richness, reality' and 'penetrating spirituality' of the Psalms makes them essential to spiritual maturing, as they contain the 'deepest expression' of God's love, 'sanctity' and 'holiness'.[128] Von Hügel suggested that Evelyn pray the Psalms out aloud but recognized that reciting a divine office was not her *attrait*.[129]

A moderate asceticism

Asceticism was not emphasized by the Baron, although he believed it was an 'absolutely essential constituent' of the Christian outlook, recognized as crucial by 'deeper' people.[130] For him, spiritual growth was incompatible with being comfortable, hence the notion of 'costing', which Evelyn recalled as one of his favourite words.[131] But it was usually expressed in small ways rather than in more severe forms of asceticism. For instance, one small 'costing' practice von Hügel encouraged was 'little renunciations' during Lent, such as giving up after-dinner fruit and book buying.[132]

Retreats

Evelyn's experience of her first retreat at Pleshey had an enormous impact on her. She came away 'tranquil' and 'surrendered' after what felt like a 'week on the glaciers – bracing, purifying and calming'. She thus told the Baron that she would like to go on retreat 'several times a year', but he replied that it should be only once yearly, as the 'more swimming in your element' you feel, the more wise to exercise 'moderation' about it.[133] Though he viewed spiritual retreats as an 'escape from racket' to 'more prayer' than usual, he was wary that directees might overdo resolutions at retreats.[134] But in 1923 Evelyn pleaded for two three-day retreats a year as she longed for 'refreshment' and being 'completely renovated' from her 'incessantly active' life.[135] The Baron agreed but warned her not to use retreats for 'elaborate' examinations of conscience or confession.[136] Once more we see him advocating useful spiritual practices but only in moderation.

Confession

Confession was another topic Evelyn discussed with von Hügel. She declared that confession tore her to 'bits', leaving her in a state of 'nervous illness' because it encouraged introspection and her natural 'tendency' towards 'self-scrutiny'.[137] In one confessional experience in 1922 she felt that the priest devoted his time to 'smashing . . . [her] up'.[138] Given the 'highly strung' and 'vehement, passionate' temperament underlying her 'quiet surface', von Hügel told Evelyn that confession was only for 'distinct and grave sins', its purpose to elicit 'some definite act or habit' of 'contrition' and 'amendment'.[139] He was adamant: 'So long as you choose to remain under my Direction you will, please, never *think* of any Confessions except . . . a simple confession of grave acts or habits.'[140] Evelyn later recalled that the Baron 'never allowed' her to go to confession, telling her to avoid 'long written out affairs', but encouraged a 'short examen' in her night prayers for a few minutes, with 'no straining' or 'scraping' the bottom of her soul.[141]

Von Hügel criticized Evelyn's test of purity of intentions as 'excessive' but recommended a 'gradual diminishing' of her faults.[142]

The cure for her excessive introspection was to 'gently drop' her 'spiritual misery' through quietly turning to God, Christ and the poor, which would 'brace' her 'finely'.[143] Evelyn came to adopt this advice, no longer interested in 'curry combings' and finding it more humbling to simply gaze on Christ.[144]

Spiritual practices when spiritually dry

Having experienced spiritual deserts, von Hügel gave Evelyn advice for coping when spiritually dry. He recommended two distinct rules for Evelyn: a 'maximum rule' for 'fair' weather and a 'minimum rule' for 'foul'. During foul weather she should practise 'morning and night prayers (with examen)' plus two Holy Communions a week.[145] When spiritually dry, she should be like crew in sailing ships when there's no wind, who mend their sails: 'drop all . . . continuous though mixed prayer' except for 'short morning and night prayers, aspirations during the day, especially acceptances of this dryness' and 'Holy Communion'.[146] Practising this minimum rule when spiritually dry would enable 'fervour' to return sooner.[147] Evelyn was also advised not to write or speak when dry but to turn to her gardening, and when busy with lectures to use her 'minimum rule', plus whatever recollection she could manage.[148]

Non-religious interests

The need to 'lovingly' cultivate non-religious interests was another major emphasis in von Hügel's direction, taken from Père Grou, and serving as an antidote to over-absorption in spiritual practices.[149] The Baron was aware that our passion for God can become 'intense' and 'over-strained', so 'sympathetic contact' with the 'homely' is necessary for developing a deepening 'transcendental sense'.[150] As Evelyn's professional work involved religion, von Hügel encouraged activities and interests of a 'not directly religious kind' – anything 'wholesome' for which she had a 'relish'; she chose gardening, book binding and script writing, finding that manual work 'steadied' her.[151] One Christmas Evelyn gave the Baron a passage from St Cyprian in half-uncial script.

Five reasons for non-religious interests were provided by von Hügel. First, if we are to 'help' others, our religion needs to be 'full' and 'mixed', or it becomes 'thin' and 'sentimental'.[152] Second, our everyday normal lives provide the material for our spiritual formation: without activities and interests that are not directly religious, we lose the 'material' for 'Grace to work in and on' and 'penetrate', thus these interests should be 'taken up' for the 'sake' of religion, alternating non-religious and religious study.[153] Third, engaging in non-religious interests ensures 'stability, sobriety' and 'genuine detachment' so we 'grow . . . more spiritual and holy'.[154] Fourth, non-religious interests help us 'escape' from ourselves as we are 'purified, trained and deepened'.[155] And, fifth, non-religious interests provide 'rest' and a chance to recharge, but the Baron's one note of caution was moderation: 'Do not have too many practices; the soul to grow needs quiet.'[156]

The importance of rest

The Baron emphasized the importance of 'rest', modelling it through his daily walk, jigsaw puzzles and cinema outings, as a safeguard against 'overwork' of body, mind and soul.[157] He also stated that Sabbath-keeping worked the 'full restfulness' for him, adding that he would 'break down in health' if he didn't stick to his 'necessary . . . rule of keeping the Sunday strictly for rest and freedom'.[158] His Sundays were for 'sleep', 'open-air strolling', 'light literature' and 'Church', and were key in 'washing' away his 'largely hurried spirit', so he could gain a 'sunny, quiet, accommodating, cheerful, grateful, great-in-little spirit'.[159]

Evelyn took on board the Baron's advice, and her Sunday routine became early morning church, then after breakfast driving with Hubert in the countryside to gaze at and be refreshed by birds, flowers and trees. Evelyn came to absorb von Hügel's attitude, describing a month of illness as 'full of a sort of leisured heaven-liness' and 'very steadying and enlarging'. She believed that through such 'leisure one *can* get quiet and recollected' and 'make 'progress'. Thus she came to recognize she would 'never seriously improve in prayer and vision' unless she could get 'stretches of quietude'.[160]

Von Hügel also helped Evelyn set boundaries so she could manage her energy. He had personally worked out 'how much' he could try to 'help others without getting markedly empty' himself, stating that when he got to that point, he politely refused to answer fresh correspondents: 'I tell them frankly how matters stand and that God will find them . . . some helper with sufficient leisure for the purpose.'[161] After Evelyn's mother died, von Hügel suggested she not take on any new direction work and postpone old cases, for 'wise living' demands 'frequent refusals'.[162] This teaching on the import-ance of rest was closely related to the Baron's leisurely spirituality.

Moderation in general

While recommending many spiritual practices to Evelyn, von Hügel also advised her to be careful about *how* she approached them, advocating a leisurely spirituality. This emphasis, imitating the French spiritual masters, came from recognizing that ardent souls are frequently too 'intense' and learning from the paradox of Fénelon's 'light, open and elastic temperament' and 'earnest will', without being 'heavy'.[163] This balance is attained through a 'genial, gentle, leisurely expansion – no shaking of the nerves, no strain, no semi-physical vehemence, no impatient concentration'.[164] Von Hügel confessed his own constant need to 'drop . . . feverishness', thus he provided a repeated cluster of instructions related to devel-oping a '*very full*' and yet 'leisurely' life.[165]

Reducing the number of activities each day

Fénelon's method of beginning each day by quietly running through the day's activities and reducing the number of them meant that each action had an 'air of leisure', which helped him retain a 'spirit of prayer and peace'.[166] Von Hügel encouraged his directees to be like Fénelon and Augustine, men of immense activity who were yet 'deeply recollected'. He said that if he woke up feeling he had a hundred things to do, he knew it was 'all wrong', and so would try to get away for a walk with Puck, leaving everything until he was 'better'.[167] The Baron's niece recalled that the 'kernel' of his teaching was 'moderation' and 'steadfastness', a 'small' but 'very faithful practice': 'do not give yourself too much to do'.[168]

One thing at a time

Von Hügel also introduced his directees to Catherine of Genoa's maxim of doing 'one thing at a time', which meant doing just one thing with 'peace' and 'non-hurry'.[169] He argued that the 'more full and varied' our lives become, the more this 'principle and practice' is needed, to 'prevent distraction and racket': *Variety up to the verge of dissipation: Recollection up to the verge of emptiness*: each alternating with the other and making a rich fruitful tension.'[170]

Slow spiritual growth

The Baron also emphasized that we must understand spiritual growth to be slow and steady. He 'disliked and distrusted hurry and anticipation – change, excitement and reaction' being his 'greatest foes'. He believed that 'dullness and routine, faithfully accepted', were necessary for the soul's growth.[171] For von Hügel, there were no easy short-cuts to spiritual maturity. He gave his directees Francis de Sales' letters of spiritual direction to Madame de Chantal as a model for spiritual growth because of their patient, slow approach, for a 'spirituality of the little-by-little' is not an 'enfeebled' spirituality.[172] Directees were encouraged to be 'patient' with themselves and to hate their personal faults in a 'calm and peaceful' way, for such steady perseverance is a 'crowning grace'.[173]

Moderation in spiritual practices

Von Hügel's leisurely spirituality was also important to moderate directees' intensity and complexity. The Baron couldn't bear the 'piling up of petty devotions to foster an extravagant piety'; he advocated 'moderation and steadfastness . . . a sober, well-proportioned institutionalism'.[174] This emphasis on moderation came from his natural temperament – his 'over-intensity' and involuntary 'over-eagerness' – which he constantly needed to monitor.[175] Just as Huvelin had helped the Baron cope with his intensity, von Hügel recognized Evelyn's vehemence as a chief cause of her instability and anguish.[176] He believed that moderation of spiritual practices would help her, for such 'simplicity' and 'singleness of spirit . . . forms saints!'[177]

From his study of Catherine of Genoa, von Hügel knew that being over-zealous spiritually could damage both one's spirituality and one's physical and mental health. He therefore emphasized monitoring the intensity of one's spiritual practice. He couldn't personally apprehend anything seriously without 'tension', which was why he had 'misgivings' when he gained any great 'influence' over others, seeing how people cannot stand much tension but either they break down physically or their 'faith collapses' owing to the 'strain'.[178] From his own experience, the Baron knew about nervous collapse; he believed that there is a 'great art' in 'managing one's nervous energy', hence the necessity for 'grand rest'.[179]

Don't strain

This idea of not straining in one's spiritual life was another recurring theme in von Hügel's direction. Evelyn was given 'suggestions' for praying 'quietly, without strain', and told to 'gently practise, a *moderate* amount and kind of *devotedness*' but without 'vehemence' or 'feverishness'.[180] Similarly he wanted to save her from 'overburdening', knowing her tendency to overdo things; he prayed that God would help her 'moderate' herself, even in 'good things'.[181]

Never fight directly

Von Hügel recommended that difficulties be dealt with indirectly by softly 'dropping' any miseries.[182] Directees were repeatedly encouraged not to fight directly or to force feelings impatiently, but to bear them 'gently', as one would a fever or toothache. They were to turn to God, not 'scratch' the itch but simply 'drop . . . non-reverberation of feeling'.[183]

Similarly, self-occupation and self-obsession were to be fought indirectly and gently. Evelyn wrote to the Baron of her 'struggle' to 'leave' all her 'professional vanity' at the foot of the cross, recognizing that unless she could do that, she might as well 'give up altogether'.[184] The Baron replied that she was being 'excessive' and should not struggle against desires, as that leads to 'strain, scruple' and 'self-occupation', but instead simply 'drop' self-absorption through turning to God.[185] The Baron emphasized that, in addition to gazing at the triune God, our spiritual formation is primarily the work of God through union with Christ and the Spirit's indwelling.

Union with Christ and human transformation

The formation of metamorphic rock was the image von Hügel used to vividly illustrate how union with Christ recreates the entire person. As an amateur geologist, he understood that metamorphic rock is formed through a process of heat and pressure slowly transforming the material on which it operates. Similarly, God 'permeates and gradually changes' the 'very substance of our humanity' through a kind of 'divine infiltration'.[186] This indwelling of Christ is a slow, progressive pervasion of our entire being – head, heart, will, emotions, body – rather than intellectual knowledge, lodged like a sedimentary layer on the surface. So von Hügel emphasized the transformative effect of the life of God slowly permeating the being of the entire person. Underlying his spiritual direction was this understanding of the penetration of Christ in the soul. Although he also spoke of the Spirit's role in transformation, at times he explicitly emphasized that 'Christ recreates'.[187]

Evelyn devoured the Baron's writings, trying to absorb his influence. For example, her 'Green Notebook' opens with her notes on his article 'Morals and Religion', and after reading his posthumously published essays, she reflected, 'what else is there left to say . . .?'[188] *Eternal Life* was another significant work of the Baron's in which Evelyn immersed herself. Von Hügel told his directees, 'I wrote the whole thing praying; read it as written.'[189]

Transformation through 'Christ–Spirit' indwelling

The biblical basis for von Hügel's *Eternal Life* was Romans 8. He described 'Christ–Spirit' as the element with which our human spirit is 'surrounded' by and 'penetrated', like the air we breathe: we are 'baptised, dipped, into Christ, Spirit' and can 'drink' Christ, the Spirit.[190] When speaking of this mystical union, von Hügel used the terms 'Christ' and 'Spirit' interchangeably. He viewed the experience of 'Eternal Life' as the 'most real of relations' between humans and God, and, rather than its being limited to a future reality, he understood it as being experienced now: 'moments' of a 'real experience of Eternity do occur, even in this life'.[191] Von Hügel described Catherine of Genoa's 'favourite teaching' as heaven beginning 'here below' and was indebted to her.[192] This indwelling is a mystical penetration of Father, Son and Spirit in the believer.

Von Hügel argued that we can gain glimpses of eternal life through engaging in contemplative prayer. At several points in *Eternal Life*, von Hügel pointed to union with God through prayer, stating that such experiences come to 'riper, deeper souls' and quoting Augustine as an example: 'we transcended our very minds . . . we touched It slightly, by an impulse of all our heart' then we 'sighed, and returned to the sound of our own voices'.[193]

But, alongside prayer, experiences of the eternal are also implicit in ordinary, everyday experiences: 'latent or patent' in every 'human

life and act'.[194] Von Hügel provided examples of human manifest-
ations of the experience of eternal life, where 'utter absorption in
God' was balanced by a sense of God's presence in souls – 'the
joyous expansion' of our entire nature through this 'keen sense and
love!'[195] For example, Mère Marie de la Providence, who led a mixed
life, was absorbed in adoration of God but also served the sick.

Cultivating eternal life

Given the central importance of von Hügel's concept of eternal life,
one of his aims in his spiritual direction was to help his directees
cultivate an awareness and sense of this abiding presence of God
as the primary means to growth. In describing the soul that 'prac-
tises' and experiences eternal life, von Hügel implicitly suggested
that it is something that can be nurtured.[196] He highlighted some
of the elements essential to the 'deepest development' of eternal life
in the believer's life: '*Duration*, history; Space, Institutions; Material
Stimulations and symbols, something sacramental', as well as
'Transcendence, a movement away from all and every culture and
civilisation, to the Cross, to asceticism, to interior nakedness and
the Beyond'.[197] Here once more, we see the Church's essential role in
the cultivation of this mystical indwelling that transforms the soul.

The effect of eternal life: spiritual formation

For von Hügel, spiritual formation was the natural by-product of
union with God. When one directee doubted the reality of God, von
Hügel asked her to look at the lives of believers and to see transformation and fruit as evidence for God.[198] However, he made it clear that
in our earthly life we can never attain our 'spiritual personality' in
its 'full beatitude', but rather that it is only 'begun' in this life, for the
'greater' has to 'awake' and 'grow within us'.[199] Rather than feeling
guilty, impatient or fanatical about his character, von Hügel accepted
that on earth he would never attain true godliness. Anything here is
merely preparatory but can lead to growth in Christlikeness, which is

revealed through a 'deep' and 'tender love and service of our fellow-creatures', acquired through 'close union with God' and produces a 'profound self-knowledge', purifying us from our 'petty self'.[200] This union with God brings forth 'continual rebirth' and 'expansion' through 'closest touch with' the 'abiding' God and is 'occasioned and sustained by' the experience of eternal life.[201]

To experience eternal life is to live a qualitatively different life. In von Hügel's words, it is experiencing 'a Living One ... Who, touching me, the inferior, derivative life' causes me to live 'by His aid' and 'for His sake'.[202] The indwelling of the triune God causes the believer to live no longer for self but for God. In fact, we find our 'true self' through this love of Christ, as we are caught up in his embrace. Von Hügel outlined seven virtues at the supernatural level that result from this union, and humility was viewed as the 'true foundation' for all of the virtues.[203]

The indwelling of eternal life also provides a double sense of reality – once more, the Baron's idea of living in two worlds. Recognizing the 'Reality of realities, the Eternal Spirit, God' behind all other realities, provides hope, joy and purpose.[204] This double sense, argued von Hügel, makes us profoundly 'incarnational' and 'real' but without 'inflation', filling us with a 'dauntless faith, courage, and joy' and a 'creaturely temper' that respects the 'body' and 'matter'.[205] Eternal life gives us a 'keen sense of His Perfection, Simultaneity and Prevenience' in contrast to our 'imperfection' and 'dependence'.[206] This transformation and essential self-knowledge through the indwelling of eternal life was a crucial concept underlying von Hügel's theology of spiritual formation and his spiritual nurture of Evelyn.

Alongside the institutional element and the mystical element, von Hügel also insisted on the importance of the intellectual element of religion. In Evelyn's case, this was not an element that was greatly emphasized, given her learning and deep immersion in wide spiritual reading. However, it is worth briefly considering some of

the main contours of von Hügel's thinking about God and the soul
and how they influenced his spiritual formation of Evelyn.

The intellectual element

The Baron made it clear that people 'must be helped' to get their
'notions' of God 'sound' and 'strong'.[207] But, while he recognized
the importance of our ideas about God, he also argued: 'Drop
brain, open wide the soul, nourish the heart, purify, strengthen
the will: with this, you are sure to grow; without this, you are certain to shrink.'[208] He recognized the importance of our doctrine
of God, focusing in particular on three attributes. He argued that
the Christian life begins, ends and proceeds with the 'Givenness',
'Otherness' and the 'Prevenience' of God, and that the 'one-sided
relation' between God and humanity constitutes the 'deepest measure and touchstone' of religion.[209] The *givenness* of God is the idea
that God exists apart from and prior to our human experience. The
otherness of God is his insistence that God is fundamentally 'other',
not an anthropomorphic deity made in our image, not simply a
'man of but larger size'.[210] The *prevenience* of God was the Baron's
conviction that God is the great initiator, whose actions always
precede human response. Thus God loved us before we loved him;
his love 'rendered possible and actual' our love of God.[211] The para-
digm of God as initiator was crucial to the Baron's understanding
of human participation. He wanted his directees to be attentive
to God and his actions, rather than to view themselves as the centre.
God is the initiator to whom we respond. Thus grace is God's 'constant prevenience and gift'; he works 'in us, not by us'.[212]

Evelyn fully absorbed the Baron's emphasis on the prevenience
of God, as revealed in her own letters of direction. She also recalled
the Baron's key words for religion as 'God–adoration–self-oblivion–
surrender' and 'transcendence' – terms that became 'incandescent
with a supernatural fire' when he uttered them; his passion was for
God, 'in Whose presence' we 'strive to grow and be'.[213]

Balancing the intellectual with the mystical

Von Hügel lived a life seeking to hold scholarship and sanctity together. The French spiritual masters of the seventeenth century had helped him to not exalt or neglect the intellectual element. The Baron similarly sought to help his directees to hold together the rational and the affections, for he had experienced how intellectual engagement can help *maintain* and enrich one's spiritual life if it is *balanced* with the mystical. He repeatedly stated that 'growth' must be a 'deepening and expansion of the whole being' – 'head' and 'heart'.[214] So the intellectual element must always be held in tension with the institutional and mystical elements to prevent faith from becoming overly rational and disconnected from the real world. This was a key aspect of his spiritual nurture of Evelyn.

The Baron warned against an excess of the intellectual element. He believed it was sometimes necessary to 'starve' a person's 'speculative bent' and to feed 'devotional needs'.[215] He had critiqued Evelyn's religion for being 'too intellectual' in character:

> You badly need de-intellectualising, or at least developing homely, human sense and spirit dispositions and activities . . . it will, as it were, distribute your blood – some of your blood – away from the brain, where too much of it is lodged at present.[216]

He also wondered if Evelyn's tendency for possessiveness in friendships – her 'tummy-ache of the soul' – was due to her over-intellectual character and emotional starving.[217] He counselled a gentle 'detachment' from particular friendships, encouraging her to incorporate more 'homely' emotions and activities into her religion to help her 'lose the hunger for the ardour of human affection'.[218] In 1922 Evelyn wrote that she still found people attractive but could now take friendships 'rather less intensely', but she recognized that she was 'still absurdly oversensitive', and still 'easily tipped off' her 'spiritual balance' through 'worries'.[219] Visiting the poor was key in helping Evelyn become less possessive in friendships and be 'de-intellectualized'.

Von Hügel encouraged his directees to have both the mind of the 'scientist' and 'religious instincts', gaining infused mystical knowledge through prayer.[220] He emphasized that the 'palace of the soul' requires 'two lifts' – one 'from below' and one 'always going down from above'.[221] But, while he stressed the importance of both movements, the lift from individuals to God was less valued than the lift coming down from above, representing truth directly revealed by God through mystical encounter.

An experiential knowledge of God given to the humble

Experience was central to theology for von Hügel. His 'supreme contribution' was abandoning an 'abstract, deductive' approach and embracing an 'inductive, experiential' method.[222] His 1906 article 'Experience and Transcendence' was where he first expressed this orientation to theological investigation. Rather than focusing on cerebral conceptions of God, von Hügel emphasized knowing God through encounter. In *The Reality of God*, he argued that we 'gain' the 'theocentric' through our 'experience', as well as our 'analysis' of that experience.[223] Given this emphasis on an experiential knowledge of God, von Hügel taught his directees about the humble, receptive posture necessary for gaining such infused knowledge. This was clearly expressed in his letter to one directee:

We get to know such realities – only if we are sufficiently awake to care to know them, sufficiently humble to welcome them, and sufficiently generous to pay the price continuously which is strictly necessary if this knowledge and love are not to shrink but to grow. We indeed get to know realities, in proportion as we become worthy to know them, in proportion as we become less self-occupied, less self-centred, more outward-moving, less obstinate and insistent, more gladly lost in the crowd, more rich in giving all we have, and especially all we are, our very selves.[224]

This humble posture is essential or we come away from study more 'rebellious and empty', 'despairing and bitter' or 'more sceptical' than we came to it.[225] We need a 'creaturely' posture that involves a relational encounter with God rather than standing above God, trying to master who he is or to delineate him definitively. Ultimately, we come to know God through loving him. Von Hügel wrote that knowing God is like our knowledge of people: 'we love . . . we develop, direct instinct and intuition' through a 'subtle and complex' process that is 'rich and vivid, but distinctly not simple and clear'.[226]

Alongside a prayerful posture, von Hügel repeatedly spoke of childlikeness as essential in knowing God. He wrote that so many people are too 'clever' for religion – we want 'less brains, more heart. Brains are no use, we want the child. I always try to get the child to come up in people.'[227] Reflecting on one of the Baron's reports, Evelyn recorded in her 'Green Notebook': *'Be . . . childlike . . .* This childlikeness confounds the wise and God Himself speaks by the mouths of such children.'[228] Evelyn came to recognize that the 'true relation' between the soul and God involved a 'simple', 'childlike dependence'.[229]

A 'dim' knowledge of God rather than 'clever' clarity

Another significant aspect of von Hügel's understanding of God was his emphasis on religion being 'dim' and requiring a 'certain contentment in dimness'.[230] He emphasized that our knowledge of God is not a 'clear apprehension of the whole' but, rather, the 'confused experience of the parts' – always a 'dim sense'.[231] He thus warned against clever people who try to invent God or define him narrowly.

By contrast, he encouraged directees to a 'frame of mind' that was 'costingly [sic] wise . . . ruminant, slow' and 'thorn-crowned', yet 'soul-inspiring' and 'life-creating'.[232] Von Hügel moved 'step by step . . . verified every shade of his meaning'; his mind accepted this 'mystical dimness' and was 'fed and enriched' through the 'perception of things' that can only be 'dimly known'.[233] Underlying this dimness was his emphasis on 'mystery' in religion: it will never be 'absolutely clear', or it's not worth anything.[234]

Von Hügel's doctrine of dimness was the reason that he encouraged his directees to a reflective, contemplative stance rather than one that is merely cerebral and dissecting. He wrote of the need to be 'silent about great things; let them flow inside you. Never discuss them', for it 'makes things grow smaller. You think you swallow things when they ought to swallow you.'[235] For he recognized that in any theological exercise:

> We are like sponges trying to mop up the ocean. We can never know God exhaustively . . . We can never picture God or imagine him. Either we make him too small, and we strain at that, or we make him too big, and he strains us . . . We shall never be able to explain God, though we can apprehend him, more and more through the spiritual life.[236]

God's great difference from ourselves means that we can 'never . . . adequately comprehend' him.[237] Evelyn recalled the Baron's 'penetrating sense' of the 'significance' of things and how they are always holding 'further depths of meaning in reserve' for us, hence his remark that if he 'cannot adequately define even a daisy', how can he understand the mystery of humanity or completely know God.[238] He argued that the 'obscurity' of his life to his dog must thus be 'greatly exceeded' by the obscurity of the life of God to him – 'so different and superior, so unspeakably more rich and alive' than his own life can ever be.[239] For, with God, we 'cannot encircle Him, map

Him out' or 'exhaustively explain' Him.[240] As such, von Hügel encouraged Evelyn to feel content with pondering dim perceptions of God and letting those perceptions grow, drawing her into adoration.

Dimness and clarity: 'get this very clear'

And yet von Hügel didn't simply leave his directees confused and swimming in a cloudy pool. He constantly balanced the necessity of dimness with the importance of clarity. Gwen Greene described how the Baron stressed this dimness, yet simultaneously urged 'get this very clear'. 'Dimness' and 'clearness' were words he often used, but Gwen reflected that generally we 'lack . . . perception' regarding what should be 'left dim' or what should 'stand clear.'[241] But she vividly recalled the areas von Hügel emphasized as needing clarity:

> most of all, we must have a certain clearness in regard to Christ, and to God. The reality of God, His nearness to us through all things, yet His transcendence of all things. Our dependence on Him and His Grace; and our illimitable need for the love of Christ. Yet clear in a kind of dim profoundness that we cannot exhaustively explore; they are dim certainties of which our apprehension grows.[242]

Thus we see once more von Hügel holding two seemingly conflicting ideas in tension, balancing a need for clarity on the essentials of faith with a dimness where those essentials shade off into mystery. But it was not just what the Baron taught about clarity and dimness that influenced directees; who he was had a much greater impact.

Personal qualities as a spiritual director

The Baron's personal qualities as a spiritual director were frequently mentioned by directees and eyewitnesses. He had 'fatherly wisdom' and a 'touching humility', radiating 'affection' with a 'warm', loving presence, 'kindness' and 'generosity'.[243] Lucy Menzies highlighted the 'gentle, affectionate care' in his letters to Evelyn, but added that he could also be 'severe'. Lucy once spoke to Evelyn about her 'severity' with her directees, and Evelyn had retorted, 'her hand in velvet glove indeed! You should see *my* old man.'[244]

Directees recalled the Baron as a 'penetrator' of the mysteries of the human heart and 'quick' to discern one's thought and to 'penetrate' the most 'delicate' shade of feeling.[245] His understanding was 'very deep', and Evelyn recalled he was able to 'enjoy small jokes'; someone hearing the laughter in one of their 'interviews' thought religion must be most 'amusing'.[246]

Evelyn emphasized that von Hügel's 'great sanctity' was full of the 'breadth', 'depth' and 'tenderness' of the saints.[247] She also highlighted his 'passionate sense of God' and 'intense interior life' – the 'awe and passion' with which he uttered God's name.[248] Directees described the Baron as a prayerful, adoring soul, with one declaring that she 'owed much' to von Hügel's prayers for her.[249] Evelyn described the Baron as a 'contemplative' and his niece highlighted how his 'significance' lay in his prayer – his 'deeply conscious concentration on, and absorption in, the Spirit of God'.[250]

Evelyn described von Hügel's gift for 'discerning spirits' which produced a 'spiritual persuasiveness', alongside his 'strongly practical bent', which was conspicuous when discussing 'institutional practices' – a quality similar to de Sales'.[251] He also operated as a fellow pilgrim who was 'truthful, sane and tolerant', relating his own life experience with 'warm', 'natural sincerity'.[252] One directee recalled von Hügel's advice as being in accordance with that of the 'great directors of the past' for he possessed a 'marvellously rich and correlated knowledge', which was rare.[253] Echoing this, Allchin recognized how the 'whole Christian tradition, wonderfully embodied' for Evelyn in von Hügel's 'person', enabled her to become balanced, calm 'safe and certain'.[254]

And the Baron suffered for his directees. He recognized that interior things cost one a 'good deal'; thus to 'help' the life of another soul means a 'specially large double death to self' for the 'life-giving soul'. This 'death to self' comes as one assesses what should be said, then anticipates the acceptance of that 'essence'. At this stage, the 'light-bearing soul' needs to help the person 'clothe the newly won essence' in clothing from *their* 'wardrobe'.[255] But von Hügel believed that such voluntary suffering for others was like 'storing up riches' for souls.[256]

Evelyn never explicitly critiqued the Baron's spiritual direction. I believe that the primary weaknesses in his approach are evident when he succumbs to values more indicative of the age in which he lived than of the essence of the Christian tradition. For example, we see patriarchal, asymmetrical influences when he asked female directees to sit on a 'footstool' or an 'uncomfortable chair facing the light' during face-to-face sessions, requesting that they do handicraft while he spoke.[257] Also, the Baron's deafness made his relating with others less dialogic, hence his talks tended to be monologues, where a key aspect of effective spiritual direction is attentive listening.[258] Given that Evelyn's direction was primarily through letters and reports, this was presumably less of a hindrance in her case.

Coda

Several commentators believe that, apart from the mystics, von Hügel was the 'most formative influence' on Evelyn's life, though others downplay his impact.[259] But, as Allchin argues, Evelyn wasn't simply a 'popularizer' of the Baron's ideas, for some of her 'distinctive ideas' and 'intuitions' were formed prior to his spiritual direction. However, I believe it's fair to say that the Baron's guidance was life-changing for her, and established the 'spiritual and theological position' she was to occupy for the rest of her life.[260]

Armstrong argued that Evelyn was not a mere 'echo' of her spiritual master, as her book *The Mystics of the Church* was not the sort of book the Baron would have written.[261] However, he also believed that the Baron 'epitomized' for Evelyn all 'she knew she was not but felt she must become', to be truly Christian and an effective help to others.[262] Geoffrey Curtis C. R. echoed this, arguing that it would be 'difficult to overestimate' the Baron's 'influence', both 'spiritual and intellectual', on Evelyn's maturer life, 'deepening, strengthening and liberating' her in the 'recovered simplicity of devoted faith'.[263] Similarly Steere acknowledged a new 'tone and focus' in Evelyn after having von Hügel as her spiritual director: 'What she learned from von Hügel's direction, she gave costingly and with a moving abandon to others.'[264]

Several commentators have claimed that Evelyn effectively diffused and interpreted von Hügel for wider audiences.[265] Cropper claimed that the Baron's 'outlook' had never been easy for English people to gain, as he 'always thought in German', but here was his disciple speaking with 'exquisite clarity' as von Hugel's 'most able' follower and impressive interpreter.[266] F. R. Barry went further, arguing that *all* of Evelyn's writings are an 'interpretation' of von Hügel, but her pen 'drives less heavily' than the Baron's.[267] In 1937, when she heard Archbishop Goodier remark that the Baron was 'better understood' through his 'interpreters' than through actually studying his writings, Evelyn responded, 'In other words, mince is easier to swallow than a cut off the joint. Well! Well!'[268]

I believe that Evelyn was in no way the Baron's clone, but that his influence was significant, as he rooted her in a solid Christocentric foundation. Through von Hügel, she encountered Christ – he 'saved' her. Olive Wyon echoes this, confident that Evelyn's 'enduring influence' was 'due to' her 'close contact' with von Hügel, who 'changed her life', bringing her into the 'heart of her Christian faith'.[269]

Resonances from the Baron are clearly evident in Evelyn's letters of spiritual direction, so we now turn to examine how she continued von Hügel's legacy.

4

Motherhood of souls: Evelyn the spiritual director

her calling . . . was in her motherhood of souls.[1]
(Charles Williams)

She was a guide who knew her mountain, and taught us that
if we could be humble, obedient and courageous it might be
possible for us also to reach the snow.[2]
(Margaret Cropper)

For over three decades, Evelyn was involved in what she called the 'care
of souls'.[3] She passionately believed that those 'on the same road' can
help one another, so she engaged in the 'deepening and sensitising'
of souls.[4] However, such help was often costly, as expressed in Sorella
Maria's prophetic words to Evelyn in 1925, 'In torment and effort to
serve the brethren', which Evelyn believed simply encapsulated Christ's
'redemptive' life.[5] But entering deeply into the lives of others, feeling
their pain and carrying their burdens, was at times incredibly deplet-
ing of her own resources. Evelyn recognized that the direction of souls
costs much and cannot be done unless directors love God and his 'deep
mysterious interests' more than their own, and are therefore willing to
'lose everything' for him, even their 'spiritual peace'.[6] She referred to
one case of direction as having been 'very strenuous', and it's clear that
exhaustion was the 'price' Evelyn paid for guiding souls.[7] Though the
Baron recognized Evelyn's vocation to 'help' souls as being 'distinctly
good' for her, he was concerned about her being over-burdened, and so
encouraged her to reduce the number of directees she had.[8]

In addition to fatigue, providing spiritual direction meant a loss of friendships. Evelyn lamented that she had so few friends. As many of her friends came to her for direction, the relationships tended to be carried on with a sense of responsibility.[9] Despite this cost, Evelyn was passionate about heeding her own advice: 'live hard with both hands, and love as much as you can.'[10] Part of Evelyn's motivation came from her desire to pay back some of the 'debt' she owed to her own spiritual directors, so while spiritual direction took her away from activities she loved, Evelyn endeavoured to live out the Baron's words: 'Caring matters most.'[11]

Evelyn's 'family'

Evelyn readily received a steady stream of spiritual directees, which took up a few hours of her time each weekday. She met them in her sitting room at home on weekday afternoons or in the conductor's room at Pleshey for thirty-minute 'interview' slots. She recorded retreat attendance and direction appointments, tracking progress and recommending retreats to some directees.[12]

Evelyn called her spiritual directees her 'Family', naming herself an 'aunt-in-God'.[13] In a letter, she described this 'Family':

> I've rather a special young person coming to Pleshey . . . a true wanderer in the jungle, hungry, intelligent . . . One of my dearest and naughtiest ones has given me a rare time of it, having tried to break away and be very bad, and had to be pulled back by invisible means to penitence and peace . . . a new case . . . a nice child who has been encouraged by silly clergymen to take her inner experiences much too seriously . . . The Family has now added to its number a young doctor, first Quaker, then agnostic, and now I trust safely Christian.[14]

On another occasion, Evelyn described an 'Infant Contemplative, a perfect pet with eyes like saucers', who asked, '*Please* will you talk to me about Union with God?'[15] Her dedication to directees is evident in her use of the possessive: 'my lambs', and 'my precious slum-saint'.[16] With similar warmth, she told one directee, 'I don't know when anything has made me so happy as your letter', while another was encouraged to 'reveal' herself, if it would be helpful.[17]

Growing confidence as a spiritual director

In 1907, when Evelyn was first asked to provide spiritual direction, she confided to Hubert that she felt it a 'horrible responsibility' and 'rather ridiculous', given she was in as much a 'tangle' as anyone.[18] Feeling as though she inhabited a 'very confusing forest', Evelyn encouraged her first directee to exercise her own 'judgment' regarding her advice, as she was simply presenting a path in 'one direction'.[19] She thought of herself as an 'improving friend', feeling her way in the dark, even describing one letter she'd written as 'stupid' and 'useless', but she gradually came to sign some letters as 'Your affect [*sic*] Director'.[20]

Twenty years later, Evelyn still lacked confidence as a spiritual director, often 'floundering' in the 'dark', blindly 'wondering' what was happening in a person's soul.[21] In 1924 she felt 'less and less competent', seeing Sorella Maria as 'much better fitted' for spiritually directing Lucy Menzies, but Maria's advice was to simply make her whole life a prayer.[22] Evelyn similarly asked Bishop Frere for guidance about giving spiritual direction, and he told her to stop focusing on her own faults and to 'reach forward', like St Paul.[23]

As Evelyn began to truly understand spiritual direction as *God's* work, her confidence grew. By 1929, she was reflecting that she just had to trust that God would 'do it through' her, and that her 'own insufficiency' therefore did not matter much.[24] She had experienced in her own life the Spirit's action – 'so gentle, ceaseless, inexorable, pressing' her 'bit by bit' towards her home.[25] More and more Evelyn focused on discerning God's work, recognizing that her direction work was 'done now by something not me, which tells me exactly what to say'.[26] Thus she recognized, with wonder, the 'quick progress' of souls once God 'lays His hand on them'.[27]

Evelyn as spiritual director

So why did so many people keep coming to Evelyn for spiritual counsel? Several eyewitnesses made similar observations, that something 'other' was experienced by those who went to Evelyn for help:[28] she 'ingeminated "Love!"' – 'Light simply streamed' from Evelyn's face, 'illuminated' by her 'radiant' smile;[29] 'New life *did* radiate' from her, as a 'channel' for God's love, flowing to other souls.[30] Rather than viewing her vocation as being that of a 'guide', Williams described Evelyn as a light to 'illuminate', though initially it 'merely shone'.[31] Evelyn emitted a feeling of 'peacefulness', and the 'impression of *light*' came into the room with her; even a stranger on a bus told her that she had the 'most lovely aura!'[32]

In addition, Evelyn had mystical authority. With a wealth of lived experience, knowledge and her practice of sanctity, she was respected, even yearned for.[33] A priest who knew Evelyn wrote that, like all 'true mystics', Evelyn spoke with authority of her search for reality, and thus people 'turned to her hungrily' for they 'sensed' something in her, giving her words 'beauty' and 'integrity'.[34] Evelyn drew on her lived experiences, knowing her country first hand, which made her an articulate soulguide, yet Evelyn confessed: 'I arrive several years later at the experience of things I said.'[35] Despite this, her 'authenticity', 'holiness of judgment' and discernment of differences in souls were significant and she clearly 'conveyed God' to directees – he was 'with her' and so was also with them.[36]

It was *who* Evelyn was that drew directees and had an impact on them. Menzies recalled Evelyn's 'great serenity', 'zest for life' and eager vivaciousness.[37] Another directee described her 'acute, penetrating and generous' imagination and 'delicately sensitive mind', while another recollected Evelyn's 'humorous and spiritually beautiful face' and 'laughing' eyes.[38] The 'great depth' of her eyes searched 'deep beneath' one and 'knew you', and her 'look of affection' was one of the 'loveliest' things about her.[39] She was approachable, natural and easy to talk to, radiated 'so serene a calm' and provided a 'firm hand held out'.[40]

Several directees mentioned Evelyn's sense of humour and rare 'lightness of touch' concerning religion and people; she 'soothed' the 'tense and over-excited' through her 'impish' humour.[41] Her playful, light-hearted, accepting spirit was evident when one directee exclaimed, 'Oh dear, I must be quite different', but Evelyn cheerfully replied, 'Must you, what a pity, I do like you so much as you are.'[42] Evelyn didn't want play-acting clones. She steered people into the 'deep waters' of the Spirit with humour and 'penetrating understanding', piercing through to the truth and encouraging directees to laugh over spiritual dilemmas.[43]

Evelyn showed a 'deep and lasting' interest in people's lives, making them feel she was their friend.[44] Having experienced 'religious loneliness' made her more tolerant of what she described as 'the ever-growing crowd of bores' who had visions and wanted to discuss them.[45] Viewed as an expert in mysticism, she was often contacted by 'strange', 'telepathic', 'over-sensitive' people who talked about 'trances' or 'cranks' who gave her mystical pictures and poetry.[46] Evelyn was clear that 'vague' spirituality provides no basis for 'progress'. By contrast, God, the soul, prayer and 'responding' to God's demands are 'real' facts – living in 'harmony' with those truths brings 'light'.[47]

Evelyn was generous. She visited Darcie Otter, one of her directees, encouraging her to write and talk about her soul whenever she wished and reassuring her, 'I shall always hold on to you as long as you want me.'[48] Other directees were similarly showered with generosity: 'you are *always* welcome . . . say when you want to talk'; 'I shall be only too delighted if I can be of any help about your prayers'; 'please do not hesitate to write again, or else come in one day for a talk'.[49] She also generously prayed for directees.[50]

Evelyn described herself as a 'paw in the dark' giving a 'very pleased squeeze' to say 'All's well'.[51] She encouraged directees to 'stick it out!' and to maintain their 'larger deeper outlook' and 'growth'.[52] One directee was congratulated for having won an 'interior battle', another was told she was doing 'very well', while yet another was congratulated for having 'held on well' during 'ups and downs'.[53]

Reviews of Evelyn's first published volume of letters highlighted her light touch' and 'non interfering nature', as she didn't 'dominate' or 'mould' her directees but helped them find their 'own way' to peace and power.[54] Evelyn's understanding of 'human needs, spiritual difficulties' and 'emotional dangers', together with her 'inspired common sense' and ability for 'gently' but 'inexorably, un-selfing souls', freed them for adoration and sacrificial love.[55]

A secure, non-directive guide

Though Evelyn was always candid as a spiritual director, she was careful not to be too directive. Following Ethel Baker's ideas concerning the 'excessive' powers of the director, she imitated the Baron's reluctance to interfere, believing that the 'object' of spiritual direction is organizing the directee's life so they can walk alone.[56] Von Hügel's maxim became her own: 'The best thing we can do for those we love is to help them to escape from us.'[57] To this end, she pointed directees to the Spirit: 'You are not alone facing this situation: God's Spirit is in & with you dealing with it too'; it's 'material & opportunity for His Spirit to work on yours'.[58] One directee was reprimanded for 'elevating' Evelyn to a 'she-who-must be-obeyed' which Evelyn believed would 'enfeeble' the directee's own will.[59] Evelyn was aware that direction can be 'dangerous', as the link between each soul and God is 'personal and individual', and thus we 'can't' prescribe definitely' for each other.[60] She was thus 'frightened' of providing 'detailed advice' if she didn't know the directee personally, as she recognized that differences in temperament meant their prayer differed too.[61]

Aware that her advice was based on her own experience, Evelyn (like the Baron) repeatedly encouraged directees to feel free to reject guidance: 'do not try to twist yourself to accept my statements'; 'exercise your own judgement'; 'throw . . . away' any advice that doesn't fit.[62] Evelyn wanted directees to trust their 'own intuitions' and to find their own voice. [63] However, at times she was more assertively directive: 'Please say the Way of the Cross at least once a week during Lent'; 'Where *had* your sense of proportion got to, when you thought you had not time for your morning prayers?'[64]

We gain a vivid insight into the nature of Evelyn's spiritual direction through two published volumes of her letters. Her correspondence was 'formidable': she was a prolific letter writer, composing letters during any free moment, whether on train or yacht or by the evening fireside.[65] We now turn to examine some of the main recurring contours in her spiritual formation of others.

Spiritual formation through letters

The publication of Evelyn's letters in 1943 led to observations from many readers. The Baron's biographer, Michael de la Bédoyère, described Evelyn as a 'great Anglican with a Catholic mind', highlighting her knowledge of prayer and the spiritual life in the 'Catholic tradition'. He believed the letters could have come from 'any equally sensitive Catholic student of the spiritual life and director of souls', and recognized that they 'clearly owe a very great deal to the inspiration' of von Hügel, displaying the same 'shrewd, tolerant, understanding explanations of God, Christ, prayer [and] the spiritual life', which were repeatedly expressed in ways that were 'specially suited' to the temperaments of her correspondents.[66] T.S. Eliot similarly described the 'shrewdness and simplicity' with which Evelyn helped support the spiritual lives of many more people than she'd have been aware of, while Charles Williams experienced her letters as a 'rebuke' to readers.[67]

As the majority of Evelyn's directees were women, most of her letters were naturally addressed to women. She had met some of these directees when leading retreats, while others had contacted her after reading her works or had been referred by Bishop Frere.[68]

Three strands of sustained correspondence stand out from the published letters: Evelyn's correspondence with Margaret Robinson, an Anglican school teacher from Liverpool who had contacted her after reading *The Grey World* (1904–1917); her letters to Darcie Otter, who lived near the House of Retreat at Pleshey (1927–1941); and a sustained series of letters written 'to a friend', published in the first volume (1923–41).

The influence of the Baron

Across her correspondence, we can often sense the Baron's influence. After his death, Evelyn felt that he was still very much 'with' her, his 'influence' still 'radiating'.[69] She kept on digesting his letters and writings and, as she nurtured directees, vivid echoes of the Baron can be heard through her repetition of words he constantly used: 'bracing',[70] 'drop',[71] 'leisurely'[72] and 'don't strain'.[73]

Evelyn often mentioned the Baron to directees. She described him as being like a 'patron saint' who can be 'relied' on to provide 'courage' and 'refreshment'.[74] She said that, as he had 'directed hundreds of souls' of different types, directees shouldn't go against his word.[75] As well as quoting and paraphrasing him, Evelyn recommended his books, assuring directees they couldn't find better spiritual reading for both 'heart' and 'head'.[76] She believed that his works were particularly helpful for directees experiencing 'disharmonies' between religion and experience, and described his essays as 'grand', adding, 'how thin and arid he makes everyone else seem'.[77] The Baron's *Essays* were viewed as 'rich and complete' with 'more to give' than the work of other writers, while his *Life of Prayer* and letters were recommended as 'spiritual food' and preparation for reading *Eternal Life*.[78] Evelyn also advocated Huvelin's 'Sayings' and her own book, *Man and the Supernatural*, which she believed owed 'everything' to the Baron.[79] She also frequently recommended von Hügel's daily readings, the *Confessions*[80] and *The Imitation*.[81] One directee, thankful for Evelyn's introduction to the Baron, wrote that no one had 'helped' her so much as a 'daily guide'.[82]

Evelyn's advice to spiritual directors

Providing 'guidance and support' for a soul 'seeking closer communion' with God was viewed by Evelyn as the most 'delicate and responsible' work and as truly 'sacred'.[83] In a lecture to Anglican clergy in 1936, Evelyn stated that, though we may feel 'insecure' when asked to guide someone who's 'far beyond us' spiritually, the essential 'safeguards' are 'confident submission' to God, 'humility', 'patience, moderation and lightness of touch'.[84]

The spiritual director's own life of prayer was viewed as the essential preparation for effective soul care, for guides can only lead people 'towards eternity' when it's a 'country' they know.[85] Spiritual directors were encouraged to set aside a 'substantial' daily time for communion with God, so they could become 'channels' for God's action, touching and transforming souls.[86] In addition, the director needs to be a 'living part' of the praying Church, 'woven' into her 'eternal act of adoration', hence Evelyn recommended 'first-hand knowledge' of the great Christian writers on prayer, focusing on their personal communion with God.[87]

In addition to having a vibrant, personal life of prayer, directors were encouraged to recognize *God's* work in formation as primary, and thus accept the responsibility to pray for directees.[88] Because God sets the pace, directors were encouraged to go slowly; von Hügel had emphatically declared that 'stampedes and panics' were of 'no earthly use'.[89] Francis de Sales' patient, slow approach was provided as a model, for spiritual directors can do 'harm' by going 'faster' than the Spirit, through pressing souls on into advanced books on prayer.[90] By contrast, directees should be encouraged to humbly practise the prayer now made possible, rather than run on ahead, and spiritual directors require a 'gentle willingness to wait', 'homely patience' and 'humble self-oblivion'.[91]

Directors also needed to deal with people in a 'spirit of prayer', not through arguments, for spiritual direction is not about imparting information but about providing 'suitable food'.[92] Evelyn also stressed that spiritual direction involves the cooperation and union with God's grace: 'Out of *your* struggles and temptations, *your* tentative glimpses of reality, *your* generous acts of utter self-abandonment to the purposes of God . . . the Holy Spirit can do His work on other souls.'[93]

With emphases straight from the Baron, Evelyn advocated that spiritual directors gain a 'twofold realism': a vivid sense of God's transcendence, presence and 'over-ruling action', and an acceptance of our 'weaknesses' and 'creatureliness' – the 'raw material' of sanctification in everyday life.[94] She had learned to move easily between the supernatural and natural planes, and alongside this 'balanced' outlook, she recognized the necessity for 'robust common-sense', a 'firm yet delicate' touch, a 'wise tolerance of human weakness' and a 'hatred of moral and devotional pettiness'.[95]

Evelyn outlined two potential 'dangers' in spiritual direction: first, criticism of 'imaginative and emotional' religious experience, instead of judging by their fruit; and, second, assuming that someone who has 'visionary' or 'abnormal' experiences is a mystic.[96] She argued that authentic contemplatives are generally 'quieter, deeper and less emotional', and make fewer demands on directors because they are humble and not 'anxious to be understood', but what they do need is reminding not to over-strain and preparation for coping in spiritual darkness.[97] From personal experience, Evelyn knew the necessity of distinguishing between 'victims' of mental illness and those who were genuinely drawn to the mystical. She advocated 'strict personal training' in mental prayer and spiritual reading to help discriminate between the 'self-deluded' and the 'genuine mystical type'; the letters of Fénelon, Jacques-Bénigne Bossuet, Francis de Sales and Vincent de Paul were recommended as models of effective spiritual direction.[98]

Attrait

Another emphasis Evelyn inherited from the Baron was the importance of our personal *attrait* – souls are never 'dittos'. Evelyn became acutely aware that each person needed to be attended to as a unique individual, and not be given one-size-fits-all guidance. She believed directors needed to recognize *attraits* and stages of spirituality and to discern spirits and needs, not generalize or apply 'stock ideas' or 'form a type'.[99] Gifted with spiritual intuition, self-knowledge and sensitivity, Evelyn was able to discern nuances in personalities, and directees were told to 'gently' follow their own *attrait*. For example, one would be reminded to take things 'quietly', given she was 'temperamentally inclined' to go to 'extremes' spiritually, while another was told that her 'intense nature' meant that some spiritual advice would 'fit' her 'case', and a different directee was informed that her 'type' of soul would *'never'* find harmonizing the different sides of religion easy.[100] Evelyn was particularly gifted in helping directees deal with excessive emotions and mortifications, given her own vehemence.

The prevenience of God

The prevenience of God is one of the theological concepts most discussed in Evelyn's letters about spiritual nurture. This idea that God takes the initiative in our spiritual formation was a foundational concept for the Baron. Evelyn wanted her directees to get into their bones the idea that the first movement of religion is from 'God to us', not from 'us to God'.[101] She believed that God is present before, during and after a spiritual director arrives at the scene, stating that if she didn't think the *'whole* of life' was the work of the Holy Spirit, she'd 'give everything up'. It was the 'centre' of her 'creed'.[102]

Evelyn passionately believed in the 'supernatural' power of the Spirit, and that we should 'pray for it, expect it and trust it', for God initiates the 'paths' by which he 'chooses to come' to us.[103] She described the 'secret pressure' of the Spirit gently 'pressing' us, God 'acting' on each soul, producing in each directee what he wants.[104] God will 'intervene' when we 'least expect it' and even 'humiliating experiences' or illnesses could be the medium for his 'moulding action'.[105] From personal experience she knew that the 'seed' God 'planted' would 'grow' at his speed, without our 'fussing', for God teaches through every situation.[106] Evelyn encouraged her directees to place the emphasis on God – '*His* work in your soul' – and assimilate the priceless art of 'letting God make the first move', for the 'initiative' lies with God and he is 'moulding and leading' as it's 'His job' far more than ours.[107] Evelyn saw her task as simply encouraging directees to live responsively to God's initiative, for he can 'do His job without us', we simply need to 'depend' more and more on him.[108]

Attentiveness to God's action was fundamental, so Evelyn encouraged directees to be 'alert', 'watch', 'listen' and 'wait quietly' to see where God 'leads' by lying still, resting in God and remaining 'docile in His hands'.[109] Being 'surrendered' would increase their sensitivity to God's 'pulls and pushes' and, rather than trying to control things, they should simply take things as they come, waiting for 'new lights'.[110] Evelyn assured her directees that God is 'making' them more 'abandoned, dependent, resigned', providing his 'grace' for dealing with the future: the take-home message was 'God is in it'.[111]

The metaphor of light was repeatedly used to signify glimpses of God's action. Evelyn warned directees not to 'strain' after 'knowing more', but to 'rest' in what they '*have* been shown' – 'dawning light can't be snatched'.[112] One 'struggling' directee was told, the light comes 'suddenly and strangely' like 'falling in love', something that doesn't happen when we're desperately trying to do it.[113] Her directees were encouraged to long for God's will, even though it may mean 'darkness', and she reassured them: 'God holds you when you cannot hold Him', so be 'supple in His hands and let Him mould you (as He is doing) for His own purposes', responding with love and trust.[114] So we see this repeated emphasis on God as the great initiator who is spiritually forming us. The spiritual director's role is simply to have confidence in God's work, provide reassurance, encouragement and discernment, and not get in the way.

Liturgy

Evelyn repeatedly encouraged directees to pray the prayers of the spiritual 'greats', finding them 'educative', for the best way to know God is to 'frequent' the company of his friends through joining the Church's 'Chorus of the Church', and thus be ushered into the 'atmosphere of eternity'.[115] Directees were repeatedly told to engage in formal vocal prayer, such as the Lord's Prayer.[116] Hence one directee who had experienced a 'severe spiritual-cum-psychological storm' was told to say a few prayers 'mechanically', for Evelyn knew from experience that even a Daily Office can have a 'curious effect'.[117] Vocal prayer was recommended for those whose prayers tended to dreaminess, who experienced strain in mental prayer and who suffered, felt dry and distracted or were experiencing spiritual convalescence.[118]

Directees were encouraged to recite liturgy aloud. Evelyn believed that the spoken word has 'suggestive power', reaching and modifying our 'deeper psychic levels' more than 'inarticulate thought', because our centres of speech are closely associated with our mental life. Thus reciting the Psalms aloud was viewed as being more significant than simply remaining in a state of prayer – as we 'cease from saying, devotion vanishes away'.[119] Liturgy also shapes our devotions, argued Evelyn, as its poetic qualities arouse our 'dormant spiritual sense', bringing us into God's presence.[120]

Additional instruction in prayer

Evelyn discovered that many directees had 'babyish illusions' and 'queer' notions about prayer, so she freed one directee from 'faintly deceptive psychic chat' and told another, 'What is worrying you isn't your prayer but the rubbish people talk about it!'[121] Evelyn provided some basic principles concerning prayer. It is not a 'science' or 'system' but a 'living . . . relationship', becoming more 'personal' and 'simple' as it progresses.[122] People should follow their *attrait* rather than 'force' themselves into any particular method, for we are called to different types of prayer.[123] Prayer is God's 'gift', not our 'work' but simply our 'response' of 'humble love'.[124] God 'gives' us prayer as a 'spiritual force implanted' by Him, enabling our 'co-operation'.[125] Further, *'consciously'* living in the 'Presence of God' is 'attained' and 'clung' to by the will.[126]

Reducing strain in prayer was a frequent theme, for the Holy Spirit 'always' works in 'tranquillity', and 'harmony' is required between our 'outer' and 'inner' life to reduce strain.[127] Evelyn recommended 'resting quietly in the Divine Presence' as 'better' than our deliberate efforts and also more humbling.[128] Similarly, she endorsed a 'gentle unforced' prayer where we 'lie quiet' before God, renouncing our will in adoring prayer.[129] She reassured one directee that 'just sitting or kneeling', apparently doing 'nothing', is okay, for it is God's prayer 'in' us as 'vessels', even if we don't feel anything.[130] Also, the best prayer type is one we feel 'drawn' to, which makes it easiest to remain with God, but feeling exhausted through prayer is a bad sign, given the fine line between one's nerves and one's spirit; the 'deepest apprehensions' of God do not cause 'distress'.[131] Evelyn recognized that a person's 'nervous intensity' can be mistaken for religious experience, thus she warned directees that contemplative prayer is more 'exhausting'; so, for health reasons, they should do less than they feel 'drawn' to and they should not *'overdo'* it.[132] Relaxation was viewed as the 'safeguard' against 'intensity' and 'monotony' in prayer.[133]

Some directees were given specific instructions about mixed forms of daily prayer, for example, an hour's prayer each morning including a New Testament reading, meditation, then 'adoration, intercession' and a 'review in God's presence' of the day's duties.[134] Another example included ten to fifteen minutes of daily prayer either 'waiting silently on Him, praying or adoring' or 'reviewing' his 'presence' during the day.[135] Removing distractions and becoming still in prayer were also highlighted; thus one directee was told to meditate on the Gospels, 'picturing the scene and herself there, looking at and listening to Our Lord'.[136] Directees were discouraged from talking about their inward experiences and comparing them with others' as it 'cheapens' the experiences.[137]

Intercession was viewed as essential to a 'daily rule' as it cures personal faults, enabling us to serve others.[138] Evelyn described how the mystics have 'deep love' and 'sympathy' with humanity, loving 'all' things with God's love; concentrating on the first commandment leads naturally to the second.[139] All 'self-giving love' is 'part' of God's love, and Evelyn argued that her directees wouldn't feel happy until they had people they *can* love without fear of disaster'.[140] When feeling 'righteous indignation', directees should mix in some 'pity' for the wrongdoer, to safeguard themselves from 'bitterness'.[141]

Meditation

Evelyn taught her directees meditation, encouraging them to shut their eyes, relax their bodies and find a 'phrase, truth, dogma, event' to hold 'before' them, 'turning it over'. As they shut themselves off from their senses, they were to 'hold onto' their idea, turn their attention 'inwards', then 'sink' downwards into silence and peace, but this was to be practised only for ten minutes initially, and not when they were tired.[142]

Evelyn's own practice of recollection each morning was also relayed. After attending to a 'short verbal prayer' holding tightly to each word, she entered a phase of 'staring' at God, which did not always come and which varied from a deliberate act of 'meditation' to 'real passivity' entirely beyond her control; striving for 'states' was not her goal, just setting aside time to simply attend to God.[143]

Suffering

Suffering was a topic Evelyn repeatedly discussed for she 'never balked' at the fact that the people who '*meant business* in religion' (her expression) were 'bound' to suffer.[144] Knowing that pain is 'plaited' right through nature and supernature, she emphasized that the normal spiritual life is not a 'pleasant Sunday afternoon' or 'feather-bed' and 'champagne' religion.[145] She was adamant that 'soft comfiness' is the soul's 'worst enemy'; suffering ensures that we don't identify 'fullness of life' with 'fullness of comfort'.[146] Her directees were not to be 'purring, like overfed cats' gorging on a 'sponge cake religion', but were encouraged to embrace the cross.[147]

She argued that suffering plays a significant role in 'purifying' and 'stripping' and is a 'normal' experience in spiritual growth.[148] The 'voyage' involves a good deal of 'heavy' weather, and thus they should expect 'grey' weather, 'storm' and 'fog', even 'intense darkness'.[149] Our 'pride' needs this 'discipline' of wintry weather and it is an 'honour' to be in darkness, rather than be given a 'night-light' like a 'nervous child'; the 'Cross' is for the 'mature', ensuring we don't remain 'spiritual adolescents' for ever.[150]

Evelyn's directees were reassured God is always 'working on your soul' through suffering, so she told them, 'all is well. It is God you want and God Who wants you.'[151] Suffering is the 'very stuff' of prayer, 'deepening' lives, and nothing suffered is 'without significance' but has positive worth from a spiritual viewpoint.[152] Our 'discomfort' comes from the 'loving but drastic' action of God on the soul and even illness can be 'enforced leisure', providing the 'medium' for his 'moulding action' on souls; but our 'co-operation' is essential – we 'bear with & for' God, our 'bit' of the cross.[153]

Acceptance was the predominant response Evelyn encouraged in her directees.[154] 'Willing' acceptance of suffering is the only way to 'tranquillity' – struggling makes it worse.[155] Acceptance can take away the 'sting', so, instead of 'being cross with our Crosses' (the Baron's phrase), we need to meet suffering with joy.[156] She encouraged her directees to 'accept' the 'deprivations' in a 'peaceful' way.[157] But this acceptance is possible only when we have a 'willed confidence' in God and 'gentle acquiescence' to his leading, apart from our desires.[158] This 'surrender' and '*willing* suffering' has to be 'learned', and some learn it through 'boredom' while others learn it through 'torture'.[159] But once we accept suffering, God's grace 'mysteriously' takes away the 'real bitterness', bringing a new 'serenity'.[160]

From personal experience, Evelyn recognized the challenges of accepting suffering – 'getting off the first few coats is very hard!'[161] So she told directees not to 'force' a complete surrender while it 'raises a tornado'. Instead, they were to 'humbly' acknowledge they needed God's grace and that they wanted to be 'taken from themselves, into His love'.[162] When experiencing 'uprushes' of 'bitter' feeling, they were to turn to other things such as 'early bed', reading, the 'flicks', 'active' work for others or anything 'fun'.[163] On three occasions Evelyn quoted von Hügel's illustration about suffering being like lying still during a sandstorm and waiting until it blows over – waiting for the Lord.[164] But she reminded directees that the final outcome of the tangle was in 'His hands' and that he would use it for the 'truest good of all concerned', so they were to try not to 'resist & *kick*' but 'surrender' to his will.[165] When suffering, a 'friendly paw' and some 'nourishment' were deemed essential, so Evelyn often invited directees to her home for a talk.[166]

The Eucharist

The Eucharist was viewed by Evelyn as the means for drawing us near to God and for receiving 'spiritual food!'[167] It was understood by Evelyn as a deep 'mystery' – the supernatural penetrating the natural world – 'grace' through the medium of '*things*'.[168] As a 'mystical continuation' of the Incarnation, it involves the 'self-expression' and 'self-imparting' of God 'in' humanity and 'for' humanity.[169] She told one directee that every time she received the Eucharist, she was 'offering' herself to 'share in the Cross'.[170] Unlike 'music, beauty and liturgy', the 'chocolate-creams' of religion, the Eucharist provides 'actual energy' and 'support'.[171] Christ comes 'into' the soul, then we 'give' ourselves to be used in 'redeeming' the world; in short, 'much' is 'done' to us through partaking in the Eucharist, whether we 'feel' it or not.[172]

Accordingly, Evelyn emphasized 'frequent Communion' as our act of 'loving obedience', though she varied her specific recommendations from as much as possible, to daily, weekly, monthly or fortnightly.[173] A 'balanced régime of sacramental acts' and loving prayer would 'nourish and deepen' one's spiritual life more than anything else.[174] When any of her 'Family' were in special need, Evelyn took her communion for them – it was a practice she inherited from the Baron.[175]

Church

Given her own history of neglecting church for a decade, Evelyn passionately encouraged her directees to become committed to institutional practices. She believed that the 'regular, steady, docile practice' of corporate worship was of the 'utmost importance for the building-up' of our 'spiritual life'.[176] Our 'devotional lives' are 'steadied' through church engagement; 'humble immersion' in the Church is required, for the 'Christian ideal' involves the 'corporate and personal together'.[177] The 'accursed' individualism of one directee was viewed by Evelyn as the 'source' of 'all' her 'difficulties'.[178] Another was told that it is as 'members of God's family, the Church' that we must fully 'belong' to him, with the additional remark, 'but von Hügel will have taught you that!'[179] Alongside community, religious institutions connect us to the historical body and the 'common life', which 'calm' and 'de-individualize' our inner life.[180]

In terms of church attendance, anything beyond a weekly service was a matter of 'individual piety'; 'perpetual' church-going and sermons were not deemed necessary, but some participation in corporate worship and some 'sacramental practice' were recommended.[181]

Rather than feeling 'hustled' into the Church, directees were supported individually; for example, a directee who was 'sensitive to beauty' and found plenty in church to 'offend' her taste was told that church is for people of 'every level' of culture, and attendance would train her in 'charity' and 'humility'.[182] For the Church is made up of loving souls who have accepted their 'obligation' to play their part in his 'redemptive plan', with all that it 'costs'.[183]

Being ecumenical, Evelyn encouraged her directees to keep their Christianity 'wide' and 'deep' rather than simply focus on practices from one branch of the Church; the 'support of the whole family' should 'feed' them, and they should take what 'suits' them, leaving the rest.[184] However, Evelyn also criticized the Church for being rarely 'sacrificial' enough and full of 'second-rate collects'.[185] Thus she also ushered directees towards the 'Church Invisible' – the wide, generous 'supernatural society' – for the Church consists of *all* souls in history and we are enriched through touch with our brothers and sisters 'out' of the body, as well as with those 'in' the body.[186]

Confession

Much of Evelyn's time was spent 'rescuing' and 'reassuring' people who had received 'idiotic' advice about confession.[187] Having herself experienced the trap of focusing on her unworthiness, she quickly discerned when someone's self-occupation was actually 'spiritual pride'.[188] She stated that once we realize we 'don't matter a row of pins, self-oblivion is within reach & with it peace'.[189] Evelyn was emphatic that the 'gratuitous eating of worms *not* put before us by God . . . upsets the spiritual tummy', and thus rebuked one directee for her 'fanciful penances for long past sins', and warned another that confession would simply increase her self-preoccupation.[190]

Alert to the pitfalls, Evelyn was firm about moderation in confession: don't focus on 'misdeeds', 'scrape yourself raw', 'meditate' on your 'discouraging condition', pull yourself to 'pieces' with 'past sins' or 'pull' yourself up 'by the roots'; avoid 'spiritual spring-cleaning' which can be 'paralysing', for 'all' introspection is a 'waste'.[191] All of these errors can lead to 'spiritual insomnia' and 'spiritual jimjams'.[192]

Directees were encouraged to 'look forwards' rather than backwards, and not to take 'variations in mood' seriously or to 'feel' their 'pulse' too frequently.[193] Instead they should simply make a brief self-examination and act of contrition and 'leave it at that'.[194] If they choose to focus on a 'fault' or 'lack', they should 'glance back over the morning' to see if they've fallen into it, make an act of contrition and then at night review the day; such an examen of conscience was viewed as 'bracing' and 'wholesome'.[195] Focusing on just one virtue at a time was necessary so that directees didn't tackle more than they could 'chew'.[196]

When approaching confession, instead of 'raking' over details, directees were encouraged to positive practices: make a general statement of 'repentance' for 'lack of love'; read 1 Corinthians 13 as an 'examination paper', write down 'chief faults' and 'sins of omission' and then confess; mortify the tongue, as it reveals our criticism of others but doesn't harm our health.[197] Directees were also taught the distinction between 'sins' and 'temperament', for confession about one's temperament merely increases self-occupation.[198] Despite Evelyn's lack of emphasis on confession, she recognized it could be 'tranquillizing' and 'strengthening' to confess and receive a priest's forgiveness, so a few directees were told to confess 'regularly'.[199]

Recommended books

Books that had helped Evelyn were recommended to her spiritual directees. Given her passion for the mystics, it's hardly surprising that she endorsed these the most. She suggested Jean Pierre de Caussade, St Bernard's *Letters*, *The Cloud of Unknowing*, Julian of Norwich's *Revelations of Divine Love* ('one of the wisest' mystics), Richard Rolle, St Teresa's *Way of Perfection*, Francis de Sales's *Letters* and John Ruysbroeck (Evelyn's 'favourite mystic').[200] Jean Nicolas

Grou was repeatedly recommended, particularly his *Hidden Life of the Soul*, *How to Pray* (in Evelyn's view, one of the 'best short expositions' of the 'essence of prayer') and *Handbook for Souls*.[201] One directee was told that the Baron thought 'great things' of Grou and 'belongs' to his school.[202]

St John of the Cross was also repeatedly recommended. He was one of Evelyn's 'most intimate friends', and she argued that he helps the 'self-stripping side' and his sayings are 'terse', 'deep' and 'daring' spiritual declarations.[203] So Evelyn sent one directee *The Spiritual Canticle*, also suggesting Teresa's *Foundations* as nobler than her *Life*; she endorsed Teresa's *Life* and *Way of Perfection* as pre-retreat reading.[204]

Contemporary books were also recommended: William Temple's *Christian Faith and Life*, *Mens Creatix* and *Christus Veritas*; *The Theologia Germanica*; *Ancient Devotions for Holy Communion*; George Longridge's *A Plain Guide to Meditation*, F. C. N. Hicks's *The Fullness of Sacrifice*, Søren Kierkegaard's *Vision of God* and Rudolf Otto's *Idea of the Holy* (which was repeatedly suggested).[205] Other recommendations included Charles Williams's *Descent of the Dove*, Dom Aelred Graham's *Love of God*, E. I. Watkin's *The Catholic Centre*, Alfred Guillaume's *Prophecy and Divination among the Hebrews and Other Semites*, Edwyn Bevan's *Symbolism and Belief*, R. J. Stewart's *Inward Vision*, Maisie Spens's *Concerning Himself* and Temple's *Readings in St John*.[206] Though she rarely recommended her own books, Evelyn did suggest *The Life of the Spirit and the Life of Today*.[207] Books about prayer were also proposed: *How to Meditate* and Jacques Maritain's *Prayer and Intelligence*.[208]

Knowing the importance of models, having taken Élisabeth Leseur as her example for how to balance home life and wider claims, Evelyn also suggested biographies: the *Life* of Charles de Foucauld and of Mother Janet Stuart, the *Journal* of Élisabeth Leseur, as well as biographies about St Teresa, St Vincent de Paul, de Foucauld, David Livingstone, St Benedict, St Bernard, St Francis, Curé d'Ars, Father Damien and Mary Slessor.[209]

Daily reading and meditation on the New Testament were recommended, for if the 'meadow is God – they include all His best grass', and thus, Evelyn argued, the more they could 'live into the Gospels the better'.[210] The Psalms were also viewed as essential 'daily food' and 'spiritual treasure' and repeatedly recommended: 'turn your Psalms . . . into prayers to regain peace'; get 'familiar with the Psalms'; read a Psalm for ten minutes each morning, read 'Psalms viii and cxvi' as retreat preparation; read Psalm 121 for 'steadying'.[211] All devotional reading was to be done 'leisurely'.[212]

Humility

Evelyn's lived example of humility was more influential than her words. She told one directee not to talk or think of 'sitting' at 'her feet', for her writing represents what she 'ought to be' but is 'not'. She declared with honesty that she was 'at the very bottom'.[213] She once remarked to Lucy Menzies that when she arrived at heaven she would say, 'Don't look at me but only at those I have been able to help to bring to You.'[214] Menzies described Evelyn as 'very humble', 'expostulating' at being 'classed with the Mystics' as she had been, and Margaret Cropper similarly emphasized Evelyn's 'humble acceptance of the Way'.[215] Evelyn's friends, the communion of saints, were 'always present' to her, providing the 'root' of her humility.[216] Evelyn viewed humility and love as the 'hook & eye' between our lowliness and the 'divine vision in the saints', thus she saw 'creatureliness' and a humble 'contrite' heart as 'everything'.[217] Gaining this 'awful sight of yourself', being 'awed & absolutely humbled', argued Evelyn, is as close as we shall get to a 'guarantee of genuineness'.[218] This 'steadfastness of spirit' comes as we recognize God's 'greatness' and our corresponding 'littleness'.[219] Humility is 'what matters', bringing 'perfect freedom', thus directees were not to be 'cocky' or 'care two straws what happens to one's self' or to be discouraged by falls, for people who have 'Self' as 'all-important' get nowhere.[220] Similarly, 'fretting' over what we cannot understand is 'disguised pride', which shuts us off.[221] Hence Evelyn repeatedly taught the 'wholesome' doctrine that the 'attitude of adoration and humility' is essential.[222]

Death to self

Death to self was another theme from the Baron that Evelyn reiterated. She saw 'self-abandonment' as the 'real answer to everything', but emphasized that we can '*never* become un-selfed on our own – it is God's work in us', for the Spirit cleanses us of our 'spiritual self-seeking'.[223] Attending to God requires 'self-oblivion', thus Evelyn chastized one directee for self-occupation and another for viewing herself as 'all-important'.[224] Knowing the trap of self-absorption, Evelyn helped directees get 'out' of their 'own light' to gain 'uncluttered' receptivity to the Spirit, and reminded them that monitoring 'spiritual progress' should be left to spiritual directors.[225]

Self-focus is 'corroding' and '*always* wrong', but self-forgetfulness is the 'greatest of graces', so directees were to 'stretch' their 'spiritual muscles' towards 'selfless joy' and 'selfless pain'.[226] Gazing at God would help 'drop preoccupation', for he 'transforms self-love' and 'self-surrender' is the 'real secret' – a longing to '*give*' and not to get.[227] In addition, 'self-abandonment' through loving all others, not just friends, 'snubs' the 'demon of possessiveness'.[228] Another way to curb self-seeking is to 'deliberately force' ourselves to do things in the 'opposite direction' – engaging in intercession and external good works.[229] Evelyn also advocated 'detachment' as the cure to 'desiring & hanging onto things' and encouraged offering them with a 'light hand', for use as part of 'God's apparatus'.[230]

Rule of life

Evelyn advocated that directees adopt a 'simple' rule of life. This included a '*definite* time' daily for prayer, spiritual reading and communion, together with acts of 'charity, self-denial, patience'.[231] Sticking to a rule of life during flat times strengthens 'spiritual muscles' so that we have enough 'grip' to continue steadily during darkness.[232] One directee was recommended a 'bracing', yet 'leisurely' rule of three-quarters of an hour of prayer and reading before breakfast, and no letter-writing after 10.15 p.m.[233] But like the Baron, Evelyn advocated moderation in spiritual practices and emphasized rest.

Importance of rest

Directees were to treat their bodies with 'respect', being 'kind' to themselves, including their 'animal part'.[234] Evelyn herself had to ensure that she didn't go 'rushing about', seeing lots of people, and so encouraged her directees to engage in 'complete rest'.[235] They were to keep their bodies healthy, as God's 'property', not doing anything that would lower their 'all-around efficiency for life'.[236]

Evelyn regularly diagnosed directees' 'spiritual fatigue', 'psychic illness' and 'strained . . . emotional apparatus'.[237] Such 'overstrain' could be lessened through 'proper recreation', 'ample' sleep, Sabbath-keeping and holidays to help moderate 'self-giving'.[238] Evelyn recognized that 'bodies and nerves' enter all our mental states, so she repeatedly advocated dropping activities to 'reduce nervous tension' and gain more 'space'.[239] When they were physically ill, directees were reminded that their souls would be 'dulled', so they should relax through reading story books.[240] In short, all 'surrendered' life requires 'balance' – even a week-long retreat requires plenty of 'fresh air'.[241]

Other advice explicitly reveals Evelyn's understanding of the interrelationship of the body and spirituality. Evelyn told one directee that she wanted her 'physically as much as spiritually . . . quieted and normalized', for the body must 'not be driven beyond its strength', so she should try a 'quieting-down process in all possible ways'.[242] Another was told of the 'psychic' and 'spiritual' side to her experiences and that the 'psychic' side had been 'too fully roused', upsetting her 'equilibrium'.[243] Evelyn recognized that the 'line between nerves & spirit is often very difficult to draw' but she believed the 'deepest apprehensions' of God are the 'quietest', bringing 'awe & abasement', not 'distress'; 'nervous intensity' can be mistaken for religious experience.[244] So directees were to try to be a 'channel', a 'spiritual Robot', engaging in practices, without involving their nerves.[245]

Non-religious interests

Non-religious interests, another practice advocated by the Baron, were encouraged by Evelyn to help directees develop and maintain balance, so as to protect their physical health. Directees were told to attend to the 'non-religious side' of their lives, keeping 'non-theological contacts and interests supple and alive'.[246] The reasons provided included rest, relaxation, getting our 'breath', 'variety and refreshment' to safeguard against 'religious intensity', as well as a 'steadying effect', aiding 'spiritual health'.[247]

Mixed life

A mixed life that is both active and contemplative, as found in Christ, was to be their model.[248] This 'interweaving' of horizontal and vertical movements was encouraged so that directees could see God present in both 'home problems' and prayer. Therefore they should not cut their connections with people, for 'action' in the public realm reveals the worth of one's prayer; those with a 'deep' inner life can best deal with the 'irritating details' of outer life.[249] Thus a balance between prayer and social intercourse was recommended, particularly for those prone to 'individualism'; Evelyn encouraged directees to try to 'see' people by 'His light. *Then* they become real'.[250]

Lent practices

The principle of Lent practices was regarded as 'bracing', but Evelyn encouraged her directees to 'quiet steady stuff', not 'startling sacrifices' like reducing sleep or getting up in the cold.[251] Instead, they should turn to God frequently with glances and phrases of 'love and trust', and be 'kind and patient' with irritating people.[252]

Visiting the poor

Like von Hügel, Evelyn repeatedly recommended that directees engage in some 'personal work amongst the poor'.[253] One directee was encouraged to give an hour a week to helping the poor, while another, influenced by pantheism, was told that 'service' to the poor would be her 'cure'.[254]

Will, not feeling

Fluctuating feelings contributed to spiritual crises for some directees. Evelyn knew this ailment and consistently emphasized the importance of the *will* over feelings. Though she tried to help people 'feel' God, believing that 'direct spiritual experience' was the 'only possible basis', she also emphasized that our feelings are never the test of religion, for experiences of God are 'beyond our control' and we must not 'go to bits' when the light is withdrawn.[255] She taught that the spiritual life is 'wholly' a matter of the 'will' and nothing to do with how we 'feel'; the 'string' in our 'beads' is 'abandoning' our will to God, not focusing on warm religious feelings.[256] She repeatedly stated that 'all' that really matters is 'holding on with one's *will*'; she advocated a 'regular act of willed attention' to God, emphasizing, the '*will* is what matters' – the 'constancy' of the *will*.[257]

Directees were encouraged to turn constantly to God by an act of the will, whether they experienced 'happy feelings or not'.[258] One directee who had 'emotional cravings' for God was reassured that they are 'natural – but not necessarily spiritual', hence her focus should be 'self-offering' as a 'useful . . . channel for His work' rather than longing for experiences of 'seeing' him.[259] Directees asked Evelyn how to pray if they did not feel close to God. She replied that it is 'not humbug' to say prayers one 'longs to feel', even though our 'emotional power fails at the moment . . . *the key of the situation lies in the will*'.[260] And, when experiencing a 'tornado', Evelyn argued, the 'real equation is not Peace = satisfied feeling, but Peace = willed abandonment'.[261] Surrender of the will was exemplified through phrases such as 'Just as you say, Lord' or 'take me and make me what you want'.[262] One directee, who was no longer concerned by her 'lack of emotional feeling' in prayer, was seen to be 'building more solidly without it' as her 'will and perseverance' provided 'proofs of love'.[263] Retreatants were told not to try to 'whip-up emotion' or be disappointed if they don't 'feel anything', for God comes to our souls to 'feed' us, not give 'sensations', and we need to offer our '*whole self*', not just our 'emotional life'.[264]

Perseverance in a 'willingly accepted obscurity, without feeling' means following the example of the mystics, who don't deal with feelings but with '*love*'.[265] Alluding to *Night of the Senses* by St John of the Cross, Evelyn wrote that, when the 'jam-jar is removed', it can be 'very bitter' to our 'babyish spirits', but it must happen if we are to 'grow up'. Being made to 'dissociate love from feeling' and to centre it on the will is the only place it's 'safe!' The feelings will come back at 'God's moment', not ours, in a 'far better, deeper form'. Such darknesses are like a mountain railway with a long tunnel where we suddenly come out a stage higher than where we entered the mountain.[266]

Visible and invisible

Following her conversion, Evelyn saw everything as 'energized' by the 'invisible', and thus she no longer merely enjoyed the visible.[267] With this, she encouraged one directee to find Jesus '*so present in the visible*' that he is 'transfigured' and the 'gap' between visible and invisible is 'closed'.[268] She referred to this 'invisible' realm as 'Eternity' in several letters. Evelyn hoped that Christmas would have a 'touch of Eternity', adding that, once we're 'adjusted' to Eternity, time can seem a bit 'thin'.[269] She described how we all possess a 'real transcendental spark' which, when awakened, can '*only* be satisfied' by God, for it belongs 'wholly' to the 'Eternal'.[270] Directees were encouraged to live 'eternal life in succession', for, once we are 'fully abandoned', the 'painful tension' between the two will 'cease', for we are adjusted to his will.[271] Another directee was told that the invisible communion of saints and all that it implies was not prominent enough in her 'creed'; Evelyn hoped another directee's 'Invisible Christmas' would be full of God, even though the 'Visible part' may be 'difficult'.[272] So we see Evelyn's encouragement to be attentive to the invisible reality of eternity.

Coda

Evelyn's letters provide a revealing insight into how she encouraged people towards maturity. One directee recalled the 'inner tranquillity' in the midst of busyness that Evelyn helped him acquire.[273] Another found her letters like a 'handsome load of coals of fire', while Menzies wrote that Evelyn 'opened windows' into the 'Unseen'.[274] Cropper recalled how Evelyn called out 'all one's best stuff with 'genuine', 'encouraging' 'affection'.[275] A different directee described Evelyn's 'methods' of direction as like a successful rose gardener, who 'tends each lovingly and carefully, providing the suitable soil for the roots and pruning at the correct time'.[276] As T. S. Eliot observed, Evelyn understood the necessity for a contemplative element in people's lives and knew how to nurture it.[277]

Evelyn sometimes quoted spiritual writers in her letters of direction, and we close this sketch of her 'motherhood of souls' with a quote she selected from Samuel Rutherford:

> Hiding of His Face is wise love; His love is not fond, doting, & reasonless . . . nay, His bairns must often have the frosty, cold side of the hill, & set down both their bare feet amongst the thorns: His love hath eyes, & in the meantime is looking on. Our pride must have winter weather.[278]

5

Motherhood of souls: Evelyn the retreat leader

> My love and blessing for your Retreat. I hope . . . you will
> begin, like the cats, to see a bit in the dark.[1]

These words from Evelyn to one of her spiritual directees were
written in 1936, her final year of retreat leading. All of Evelyn's
books in her final fifteen years of life (except *Worship*) were based
on her yearly retreat talks. She was a pioneer in retreat leading in the
Church of England and helped 'invigorate' the retreat movement
between the two world wars.[2]

In 1922 Evelyn attended her first retreat at Pleshey. Initially she
was alarmed at the idea of silence and the 'mysterious peace and
light distilled by it', but she also experienced 'absolute distress'
when it ended and 'clatter began'.[3] The retreat gave her a feeling of
'belonging' to the Christian family and she returned 'tranquil',
having experienced the space, stillness and quiet of retreating.[4]
The following year she described a retreat she attended as having
a 'wonderful tuning up effect; revived love all round', with prayer
becoming more 'wonderful'.[5] A private yearly retreat became an
essential part of Evelyn's life, so when she was asked to lead a retreat
at Pleshey in 1924, her face lit up. Conducting retreats was something she had 'longed' to do.[6]

Retreat locations

The House of Retreat in the thatched village of Pleshey, near
Chelmsford, was the main location for the retreats Evelyn led from

1924 to 1936. It was originally a nunnery built on 'holy ground'; a chapel dedicated to the Holy Trinity was built on the site in 1394. Prayer had been its life for six hundred years and the atmosphere invited deep communion with God, thus Evelyn's beloved 'Pleshey' became 'more dear' to her than any other 'holy place'.[7] She described the newly built chapel, consecrated in 1933, as most 'beautiful and simple' – 'born full of the spirit of prayer'.[8] Evelyn's Donatello 'Madonna' plaque still stands in the chapel as her memorial.

Pleshey also attracted Evelyn because it possessed a homely 'normality'.[9] The rambling gardens with paths and private, peaceful spots to sit and pray, plus its proximity to quiet fields for walks, made it especially suitable as a retreat venue. Other locations where Evelyn led retreats included St Michael's House (Wantage), Little Compton, Watermillock (Lake District), Leiston Abbey, Glastonbury and Canterbury.[10]

Initially, Evelyn gave seven retreats a year, but they were later reduced to five. Three of these yearly retreats were held at Pleshey: at Passiontide, the Sunday after Ascension, and at All Saints'.[11] Evelyn gave a lot of herself as retreat conductor and described her state afterwards as a 'mental and spiritual coma'.[12] She preferred a small group of no more than twenty-four retreatants. Though she used the same set of talks for all her retreats in a calendar year, new retreats meant more people to pray for, write to and possibly direct. Though Evelyn led retreats from 1924 to 1936, it was in the 1930s that she viewed her primary work as retreat leading and the 'after-care' of participants through spiritual direction.[13] She also led 'quiet days', using three addresses from her retreat in that year, but she found these events too short and not enough detached from ordinary life to produce 'much effect'.[14]

In 1935, Evelyn took a year off leading retreats to focus on writing *Worship*. She cheekily stated that she hoped that decision wouldn't make people think she'd converted to Catholicism or had had a mental breakdown.[15] The only retreat she gave that year was one at Pleshey at Ascensiontide for her regular retreatants, with four retreat talks based on material from her book concerning the Eucharist. On that occasion, participants were also invited to stay an extra day to talk in the garden.[16] By 1936 ill health started taking its toll and Evelyn gave only three retreats, cancelling another three because of her asthma. By 1937 she had to stop retreat leading altogether. In 1938 she planned to give interviews and lead meditations at a retreat, with a priest giving the addresses, but was unfortunately unable to attend as she was confined to bed for weeks.[17] Giving up work she loved and passively accepting God's action caused Evelyn much suffering, so she tried to ponder the 'active side' of this imposed 'inactivity'.[18] While finding it 'difficult' to 'lay down tools', she understood it to be the very 'essence' of the cross and was drawn 'nearer' to Christ through having to quietly accept that a job she had been 'managing excellently' was taken away.[19]

By the summer of 1939 Evelyn had formed a small group of women who had previously been her retreatants. The group had begun in 1937, after one of Evelyn's cancelled retreats when her friend Agatha Norman gave the women some theological study. In 1939 they asked Evelyn to give them instruction on the 'devotional side' to balance their studies. Always believing that theology and prayer go together, she was happy to help. Following three face-to-face meetings, the group was scattered geographically when the Second World War began, so Evelyn continued with the spiritual formation of this small group via letters.[20] At all the great feasts of the Church she sent a letter to the group members, with the final one sent a month before her death. It was her final formation work.

Carried by a community of prayer

All the retreats Evelyn led were covered by prayer. Each spring she sent a typed slip with the year's retreat dates, asking her close friends to pray.[21] For Evelyn's first retreat, she had a 'tremendous circle praying': Sorella Maria 'prepared her soul', while the Baron told her to concentrate on 'knowing and entering into each individual soul' and its 'needs', even during addresses, not simply to impart information but to have a 'caring for' and 'understanding' approach.[22] Evelyn felt 'surrounded and supported by *something* which carried' her 'steadily' right through the retreat and 'told' her 'what to say' in interviews and 'how' to do the prayers with 'effect'. She felt that she was a '*tool* used by this strong unwavering power', that her whole 'horizon' was 'enlarged and clarified' through the experience, and thus she returned with 'immense peace'.[23]

Following that initial retreat, Evelyn had found a new vocation. From being a scholar writing about the mystics, she shifted seamlessly into leading retreats for lay people. After her second led retreat, she reflected that she could feel Lucy Menzies, the Baron, Gwen Greene and Mrs Rose with their 'dynamos turned on and helping'.[24] At times Evelyn also asked spiritual directees to pray for retreats, as this sense of spiritual accompaniment and being enveloped in prayer was essential to her. She reflected, 'it isn't oneself that does it, just as in some queer way it isn't oneself that prays'.[25] In 1932 Sorella Maria spoke of having 'suffered greatly' for the three days of Evelyn's retreat, particularly the final evening, and she hoped her suffering had 'availed for a blessing'.[26] It was at this retreat that Evelyn had the Blessed Sacrament on the altar the entire time, but found the 'white eternity . . . overwhelming', reflecting that it seemed to make 'noisy nonsense' of everything she tried to say.[27]

Evelyn loved leading retreats. The second retreat she led was more like having a retreat than giving one; then the next year she described Pleshey as 'heavenly', full of bird-song and she returned feeling 'better in body' for it all.[28] On another retreat she described the 'splendid set' and 'full flavour' as perpetually 'turned on', thus she had nothing to do but 'swim along'.[29]

Some retreats, however, involved more personal cost. One retreat she led was 'terrifically heavy', as no one had 'much lift', so she was 'hauling along sacks of spiritual potatoes' and left feeling 'depleted'.[30] A rich ladies' retreat, full of 'hard boiled Christians' similarly consisted of 'hauling them into position' all Saturday, but fortunately, on the Sunday, they went along 'under their own steam'.[31] When she was leading a retreat, it was always impossible for Evelyn to get enough time to herself.[32]

At retreats, she identified herself with her flock, sharing with them the path she was currently travelling and placing her discoveries on this journey at their disposal.[33] Cropper recalled Evelyn's face expressing her meaning so 'enchantingly', finishing a sentence with a 'fearfully disconcerting question', thrown out with a 'toss of the head' and a 'half laugh'. Her 'clear, expressive' voice was easy to listen to, her illustrations clear and her 'searching' eyes and look of affection completely 'authentic'.[34] Evelyn gave retreatants an encouraging, warm smile as she passed them in the beautiful garden at Pleshey.

The nature of Evelyn's retreats

An intimate window into Evelyn's retreats is provided by Lucy Menzies who, as Pleshey's warden (1928–1935), observed and attended them. Preparation for Evelyn's retreats began months in advance, ensuring that everything helped 'focus' retreatants' attention on God.[35] Though she took her preparation seriously, Evelyn was adamant that retreats owe 'very little' to their conductors but a 'great deal' to the retreatants' 'dispositions'.[36] However, she also recognized that the retreat conductor's 'interior life' with God had a great impact on both leading and the atmosphere created.[37]

Evelyn would arrive a day early to organize details such as suggestions for Bible reading, interview sign-up sheets and 'Points for Meditation'. She carefully selected hymns for the hymn sheet and prepared the daily Holy Communion, generally taken by a chaplain. A verse, poem or image was often pinned up on the chapel porch noticeboard, for example, inspirational quotes, a John Donne poem, a letter from the Abbé de Tourville concerning retreats and a picture of the Good Shepherd.[38] Evelyn even allocated rooms, having named the rooms as well as specific parts of the chapel – the altar, for example, was 'Adoration', and 'Compassion' was where confessions were heard.[39]

Evelyn's retreats generally ran from Friday evening to Sunday afternoon. The 'threefold bell' rang before services, reminding retreatants of the Trinity.[40] Menzies recalled the 'expectancy' in the chapel the first night, when Evelyn's voice 'broke the stillness' with her first address; she was generally the last to leave the chapel, long after retreatants had retired to bed.[41]

A page from the House of Retreat timetable is typical:

8:00 Holy Communion
8:45 Breakfast
10:00 Address
12:30 Prayers
1:00 Lunch
2–4:30 Rest and Recreation
4:30 Tea
5:00 Address
7:00 Evensong
7:30 Supper
8:30 Address
Compline.[42]

Evelyn's retreat talks usually contained between six and ten topics. The first address was given on the Friday night, reminding retreatants of the purpose of retreats and helping them enter the silence. Following that session, retreatants were given a hand-out with prayers, Bible verses, quotes from spiritual writers and thoughts for their times alone in silent prayer.[43] Three addresses generally took place on the Saturday, then two or three on the Sunday, depending on the number that had been prepared.[44] Preparatory worship through singing carefully selected hymns and the reading of prayers took place in the chapel before the address, which was followed by half an hour of silence for prayerful reflection and assimilation. Retreatants were free to leave the chapel when they felt ready. The worship services and addresses were viewed by Evelyn as the 'machinery' of the retreat, supporting the 'deepening communion', though she would add casually that retreatants were to 'take' what 'helps' them and 'leave the rest', that is, feed only on what 'nourishes'.[45]

At 12:30 p.m. on the Saturday and Sunday, a guided meditation on a New Testament passage was led by Evelyn in the chapel. Between 2 p.m. and 4:30 p.m. on the Saturday retreatants were given free time for rest and recreation, but the attitude of silence was to be maintained. Retreatants generally went on quiet walks, rested or had an 'interview' with Evelyn. The overall structure of each retreat was divided into periods of meditation, prayer, reading, worship and addresses. But Evelyn reminded retreatants that the schedule was only a 'skeleton timetable', and that they should not break off a fruitful time of prayer because it was time for something else. On the final day, retreatants were encouraged to record the 'fruits' of their retreat.[46]

Interviews

Evelyn gave 'interviews' twice a day during retreats. These half-hour-long spiritual direction sessions were held in the Conductor's Room on the first floor at Pleshey. Evelyn was present to 'help . . . suggest . . . listen' but careful not to 'press' people towards 'special paths', for there are 'one thousand ways to God', so she tried to stay 'radically open to divine initiative'.[47] Cropper recalled the 'bracing self-less counsel' Evelyn gave, constantly bringing people into 'communion with God . . . It was no guesswork with her'.[48] Transformations occurred, such as a woman gaining peace in 1933, following months of 'misery and self-reproach' concerning her husband's sudden death.[49]

Meditations

Evelyn described meditations as a technique leading to prayer that turns our minds, hearts and will 'towards God', enriching our communion with him.[50] In writing her meditations, she used Scripture like poetry, emphasizing its 'suggestive power' and opening a path into the presence of God. She encouraged her retreatants to imagine the scene, 'stay quietly and gaze at the picture and watch and listen', realizing that it is being said to them personally.[51] Her published *Meditations and Prayers* include 'The Rich Young Man', 'Emmaus', 'The Washing of the Feet', 'The Temptation', 'The Brooding Spirit of God' and 'Light'. At one retreat, Evelyn encouraged her retreatants to read a New Testament passage and to imagine the words being said to them:

> Enter the picture which the words paint, and humbly kneel within it. There let His overshadowing love teach you. The Spirit of Christ speaks to you. Open your eyes and look at Him. Open your ears and hear what He says . . . resolve to act on the light you have received.[52]

In a way that is reminiscent of Ignatian meditation, retreatants were encouraged to use their imaginations and senses to picture the scene and prayerfully enter the biblical narrative with their whole being.

Prayers

Evelyn had a handwritten book of prayers with her on every retreat and she read from this volume when leading worship. This compilation of prayers, published as *Evelyn Underhill's Prayer Book*,[53] includes prayers from women and men from all branches of the Church from the third to the twentieth centuries, with the greatest concentration in the sixteenth century. Charles Williams recalled how each new prayer Evelyn discovered from her wide reading was on 'probation' as she experienced it in prayer, before admitting it to her 'collection'.[54] The two original handwritten prayer books have crossings out and alternative options for wording, revealing how Evelyn adapted her prayers for specific retreats. For example, in Prayer 94, she changed a word to 'peace', adding the heading, 'Patience', presumably adapting it for her 'Fruits of the Spirit' retreat. She recorded the numbers of prayers for inclusion at the beginning of retreat talks using the reference 'P.B.'.[55] Towards the end of the second book of prayers, many more of Evelyn's own prayers were included in her collection, perhaps indicating her growing confidence as a retreat leader.

Hymns

Evelyn chose hymns for her retreats that were generally related to the retreat theme. Two favourite hymns were 'Love of the Father' and 'How shall I sing that Majesty'.[56] She disliked hymns that encouraged what she called 'psychological sin' – a 'childish weakness and love of shelter and petting' or a 'morbid preoccupation' with guilt.[57] She favoured hymn lyrics that helped shift the retreatants' gaze from themselves to God.

Eucharist

The Eucharist was described as the 'heart' of Christian 'worship', providing 'strength, consolation and peace', and so was generally held each morning on the retreats.[58] Evelyn argued that when we participate in the Eucharist we 'unite' ourselves with Christ's 'self-giving action', and thus are 'made' a bit more fit to 'mediate' his generous love to others.[59]

Retreat themes

Evelyn's retreats generally had one overriding metaphor to drive home her teaching. Menzies described the small, black notebooks that travelled everywhere with her and in which she jotted during quiet moments.[60] Thus we see how her retreat talks were written within the context of her everyday life experiences and prepared over a long period of prayerful reflection.

Table 1 shows the titles, dates, publication details and chapter titles of Evelyn's published retreats. In *The House of the Soul*, Evelyn described the 'ground floor' as the 'natural' life, and the 'upper floor' as the 'supernatural' life – our 'capacity' for God – which is most important. In *Light of Christ* she led her retreatants on an imaginary pilgrimage around Chartres Cathedral's windows, highlighting how the 'Absolute Light' shines through the windows of the 'different mysteries' of Jesus' life.[61] *The Mount of Purification* – originally named *Purgatorio: Seven Deadly Sins and Contrary Virtues* – was based on Dante's image of purification as climbing a mountain. In *The Mystery of Sacrifice,* Evelyn explored the eucharistic rhythm of offertory, intercession, consecration and communion. *Abba* was a set of talks on the Lord's Prayer, while *The Fruits of the Spirit* reflected on Galatians 5. *Concerning the Inner Life* contained Evelyn's addresses to priests on prayer and spiritual direction. One reviewer described it as requiring 'rereading' as it revealed the fruits of a 'life too rare'.[62] *The School of Charity* examined the Nicene Creed and was chosen as the bishop of London's Lent Book in 1934. *The Golden Sequence* was based on Evelyn's retreat talks on the hymn 'Veni, Sancte Spiritus'. Though less accessible than some of her other retreat talks, its publication meant the most to Evelyn, as the talks represented the 'precipitation' of all she'd gradually come to 'think, feel and know' and 'live through'.[63]

Table 1 Evelyn's retreat talks

Title of retreat	Date	Publication	Chapter titles
Sanctity: The Perfection of Love	1924	The Ways of the Spirit (1990)	Love; Joy; Peace; Prayer; Communion of Saints; Growth; Service; Worship
The End for Which We Were Made	1925	The Ways of the Spirit (1990)	Preparation; God; Soul; Election; Creative Personality; Prayer and Adoration; Charity

Title of retreat	Date	Publication	Chapter titles
Concerning the Inner Life	1925	1926	No chapter titles
The House of the Soul	1926	1929	No chapter titles
Inner Grace and Outward Sign	1927	*The Ways of the Spirit* (1990)	Courage; Generosity; Patience; Adoration; Communion; Cooperation; Peace
The Call of God	1928	*The Ways of the Spirit* (1990)	Vision; Penitence; Consecration; Members of Christ; Children of God; Inheritors of the Kingdom of God
The Golden Sequence	1930	1932	Spirit; Spiritual Life; Purification; Prayer
The Mount of Purification	1931	1960	Preparatory; Thanksgiving: Pride and Humility; Sacrifice: Anger and Tranquillity; Communion: Envy and Charity; Commemoration: Avarice and Generosity; Mystery: Greed and Detachment; Sloth and Zest
Light of Christ	1932	1944	Preparation; Incarnation and Childhood; Christ the Teacher; Christ the Healer; Christ the Rescuer; The Cross and the Sacraments; The Glorified Life

Title of retreat	Date	Publication	Chapter titles
The School of Charity	1933	1934	I Believe; One God, Creator; One Lord; Incarnate Crucified; Gloried; Spirit; Church; The World to Come
Abba	1934	1940	The Father; The Name; The Kingdom; The Will; Food; Forgiveness; Prevenience; Glory
The Mystery of Sacrifice	1935	1938	The Preparation; The Oblation; The Consecration; The Communion
The Fruits of the Spirit	1936	1942	Preparation; Joy and Peace; Long-suffering and Gentleness; Goodness and Faithfulness; Meekness and Temperance
The Spiritual Life	1936	1937	What Is the Spiritual Life? The Spiritual Life as Communion with God; The Spiritual Life as Co-operation with God; Some Questions and Difficulties

Four sets of unpublished retreat addresses were found without titles at Pleshey in 1990, so Grace Adolphsen Brame named them on the basis of their overarching themes. The retreat talks published as *Sanctity* discuss our holiness as a tool to be used by God, as embodied in love, joy and peace, and useful for prayer, service and worship. *The End for which We Were Made* was based on sayings from St Ignatius of Loyola. *Inner Grace and Outward Sign* provided encouragement to authentic servanthood summarized as courage, generosity, patience and other attributes. (Retreat notes taken by Darcie Otter indicate that this retreat was entitled *Three Christian Fundamentals*.[64]) *The Call of God* outlined Evelyn's reflections on Isaiah's vision. We have no record of Evelyn's retreat talks for 1929, though letters to Darcie Otter confirm that she led a retreat at Pleshey in May that year.[65] Evelyn also gave addresses for the Association for Promoting Retreats that year and spoke to the Mothers' Union earlier concerning the value of retreats.[66]

Menzies described Evelyn's retreats as full of 'life', 'zest' and 'humour' but also a 'serious matter'.[67] Cropper recalled the laughter in the chapel, and retreatants mentioned the 'delicious shafts' of humour and 'quick witty phrases' that 'lightened' the depth of Evelyn's teaching.[68] Humour drove home the deepest spiritual truths; after letting a 'particularly devastating remark' sink in, Evelyn would lighten the mood, piercing the heart by looking up and murmuring, 'How do you feel about *that*?'[69]

The purpose of retreats

A recurring theme across many of Evelyn's addresses was the purpose of retreating. Retreats are about 'communion' with God, 'self-loss' in him, so that intercession afterwards is more powerful.[70] On retreats we give 'attention' to God – the primary religious act – hence Evelyn's retreat motto was 'God only God in Himself, sought for Himself alone'.[71]

Von Hügel's description of humanity as 'incurably amphibious', belonging to both visible and invisible worlds, became a basis for Evelyn's understanding of the purpose of retreats.[72] Retreats involve withdrawing from our 'visible' environment so we can attend to our 'invisible' environment – to God – and 'adjust ourselves better to Him'.[73] Evelyn believed that, as we surrender more to God, this dualism is reduced. She argued that the distinction between the 'practical', visible life and the 'spiritual', invisible life is 'false', as each constantly 'affects the other', for we are creatures of sense and spirit. Evelyn believed that our conflicts and difficulties result from trying to 'deal' with the spiritual and practical aspects of our life 'separately' rather than as 'parts of a whole'.[74] A retreat should send us back with 'determination' to maintain a 'better balance' between our visible and invisible lives, helping us to 'redress' the 'balance' and to find the 'inward in the outward'.[75]

Retreats are for 'quickening' prayer lives and 'deepening' commitment.[76] They provide a 'pause' so retreatants can 'look across the valley' to the 'great spiritual snowfields', setting their lives to that 'great melody' and receiving 'spiritual food and air'.[77] Retreats provide a 'spot of re-birth' of our spiritual sense – a 'quickening' of what has grown 'dull and dead' in us – gaining 'light and air'.[78] In life's busyness we forget the 'awestruck upward glance', and so lose 'proportion', becoming 'fussy' and 'restless', our prayers just 'supernatural shopping lists'.[79] The 'demands' of the 'social machine' make us this-worldly and we forget our true relation to God as our religion becomes about 'doings' rather than 'attachment'.[80] Retreats redirect and recapture our 'balance', for it is impossible to serve others unless we are 'fit' and 'sensitive' to God; they are 'spiritual welfare work' and should be taken yearly to keep the soul's relation to God in the foreground.[81]

Retreats are also about the 'production, fostering and maintenance' of 'sanctity'. This 'disposition' is most easily produced by removing our 'preoccupation' with 'distractions', so we can 'attend to and realize God'. This 'in essence' is a retreat; removing life's 'pace and noise' to realize our 'spiritual status' and the 'chasm' separating 'deep' from 'distracted' prayer. For it is challenging under everyday conditions to 'learn and maintain' the 'art of steadfast attention' to God.[82]

Another description of the 'perfect' retreat is outlined by Evelyn through the French mystic Lucie-Christine, who declared: 'My soul opened and drank in God, and He was to me Light, Attraction, and Power.'[83] Evelyn 'unpacked' this as meaning that our minds are enlightened, our hearts attracted and our wills given new power – our 'whole nature' responding to God.[84] Retreats provide an opportunity to 'think', 'meditate' and 'feed our souls on spiritual food', 'deepening . . . our *whole* life' in God.[85]

Retreats are also a good time to identify the best 'rule of life'. Such a rhythm was viewed by Evelyn as one of the best ways of acquiring 'spiritual grit'.[86] She recommended a 'balance' of 'prayer, spiritual reading, work, recollection, recreation and rest', particularly emphasizing rest for balancing prayer.[87] Another aim of retreats is being refreshed from tiredness and strain and being fed so that we can more effectively 'bear challenges' afterwards.[88]

Silence and retreating

Silence was a key component of Evelyn's retreats. She playfully joked that one value of a retreat is that 'no one can speak to you!', but she constantly observed how two days of silence worked 'miracles'. Retreatants were encouraged to 'treasure' the silence as doing 'far more' for their souls than her addresses, which were the 'least part', simply indicating how to 'best use' the quiet.[89] Silence was viewed as the 'very heart' of a retreat, enabling 'inward stillness', so God can mould us; cutting distractions so retreatants could hear God's 'whisper'.[90] As God's voice is so 'still' and His deepest contacts so 'imperceptible', silence was viewed as essential, helping us 'readjust our balance' and 'attend' to what we usually miss.[91]

But silence is more than simply 'not-talking'. It's a 'complete change' in how our minds are used, and 'nothing' improves our active work more than 'quietude', a sense of 'eternity', and 'restful reception' of the Spirit.[92] A lack of 'inner stillness', suggested Evelyn, is why most spiritual lives are so 'crude', 'shallow' and 'vague'.[93] She encouraged retreatants to extend the retreat's 'holy silence' by going for afternoon walks alone, 'silent with nature', but Evelyn was flexible – if they needed to talk, they were to do so. What was key was that they avoid any feeling of being 'imprisoned' or 'strain[ed]'.[94]

Christ focus

Retreating is not just about listening but about engaging all our senses in attentiveness to God. Thus retreatants were encouraged to 'gaze' on God, leaving their 'stodgy, vague, twilit inner life' and entering the silence to gain more 'Light, Life and Love'.[95] They were drawn into contemplation – a 'fresh, intentional . . . loving gaze' at Christ's life; not for 'information' but to '*look* more deeply' with 'incredulous awe and love' and 'breathe' in Christ's presence.[96]

Using the analogy of a concert where divine music is played, Evelyn asked what gain comes from meditating on how badly we play the music. Rather, retreatants were to listen to and adore the 'harmony' offered by Christ. As they 'bathe' in 'His light', they will recognize the Spirit's 'perpetual moulding action' on their souls.[97] If they want to love and adore more, they must 'look' at Him 'more', so they become more 'sensitive' to the 'music of eternity'.[98]

Not self-focus

Across her addresses, Evelyn repeatedly insisted on avoiding self-focus: 'all self-occupation checks development'; we 'can't grow' until 'self-sufficiency' is 'dead'.[99] Even 'religious self-interest' can cause the soul's 'steady shrinking' towards 'self-love, self-will and self-interest'; self-occupation with our sins causes 'decay' in our spiritual lives.[100] Instead, retreatants were encouraged to imitate Christ, who engaged in 'self-giving', not 'self-analysis', and the saints, who displayed a passionate interest in God and others, 'not self'.[101] A 'ceaseless death to self' is what is asked of all 'light-bearing souls', rather than examining one's own state through 'self-scrutiny'.[102]

Instead of self-focus, Evelyn's retreatants were encouraged to gain St Teresa of Avila's 'self-knowledge' – a humbling knowing of self in the light of God's majesty. As we gaze at Christ, 'bathing' in his 'Eternal Light', we find ourselves 'shrinking by contrast', becoming 'as little children', and 'nothing could be better than that!'[103] Our 'little pretensions . . . shrink', we realize our 'own place', recognizing what 'mere crumbs' we really are.[104] Truly seeing ourselves in this atmosphere of 'reality', perceiving our 'inadequacy', makes God's action 'possible'.[105]

Adoration of God enables us to recognize our 'tininess' and 'nothingness' against God's greatness; the 'utter difference' in 'kind' between the infinite and finite.[106] This 'adoring gaze' as tiny creatures is how the 'entrancing beauty and pathos' of Christian prayer is 'born'; we gain a 'deepened, enriched' sense of God, becoming 'small and humble' as we fully recognize the gap between Creator and creature.[107] This 'crucifixion of self' is essential, for God uses us, his 'loving tools', in 'proportion to the degree of our self-abandonment'.[108]

Evelyn stated that the 'prevenience' of God and 'adoration' of God are the 'dominant' factors in our lives of prayer.[109] She outlined four principles essential for healthy religious living: adoration, spiritual reading and meditation, recollected prayer and intercession.[110] Echoing these principles, Jean-Jacques Olier's three headings (borrowed from Pierre de Bérulle) of 'Adoration, Communion, Co-operation' were viewed by Evelyn as the best definition of the spiritual life. Not surprisingly, we find this triad reiterated in several retreat talks, though sometimes adapted as adoration, awe and service.[111]

Adoration

'Adoration' is the word Menzies believed summed up the heart of Evelyn's teaching.[112] Evelyn defined adoration as turning to God '*for Himself*', not his gifts; 'caring for God above all else'.[113] She argued that prayer must 'begin, end, and be enclosed' in that 'atmosphere of adoration' as it is essential for developing 'wonder' and 'mystery'.[114] Without adoration we lose 'all sense of proportion' and our souls 'contract'.[115]

Evelyn critiqued the way in which churches usually emphasize service first, arguing that service will never be 'right' if adoration isn't in place, for we must first be 'receivers' of God's grace before we can be 'transmitters'.[116] Only as our souls are 'slowly flooded' by his Spirit and 'filled' to the 'brim' can we can offer 'spiritual gifts' to others and intercede 'well'.[117]

She also viewed adoring prayer as the remedy for the 'desperate spiritual exhaustion' experienced by many religious workers; when feeling 'anxiety, starvation' or 'stress', they needed to 'redress the balance' by gazing at the stars.[118] Establishing the fundamental relation with 'Eternal Reality' was essential so their prayers drew people to God, rather than relying on their own 'self-giving' and 'forcing'.[119]

Communion

Communion (or awe) is the second aspect Evelyn viewed as lacking in much contemporary worship. She was scathing, arguing that much of our religion keeps its eye on 'humanity' not 'Deity', but this 'shallow, social type' of religion 'does not wear well' when we experience 'pain' or 'mystery'.[120]

By contrast, communion is the sense of 'intimacy and love' that comes as we experience God's otherness in adoring prayer.[121] Evelyn urged retreatants to the 'humblest awe' of God, who is 'immeasurably beyond us', through having a 'contemplative colour' in their prayer life, so that they are 'rooted', 'grounded' and resting in him alone.[122] She encouraged them to draw spiritual energy from God's 'supernatural source', feeding on the 'Changeless Eternity', having 'awed' thoughts about God and our corresponding 'tininess', and to cultivate a sense of God's 'profound mystery', helping maintain this awe.[123]

Co-operation

Co-operation is our active practical 'self-giving' to God as 'co-workers' for his purposes of *redemptive love*.[124] Evelyn repeatedly reminded retreatants that the full prayer life 'swings to and fro between adoration and action', representing the Martha and Mary of their interior lives; from gazing at Christ, they must love others, incarnating his 'all-generous', 'redemptive spirit'.[125] Evelyn argued that our love towards the seen will be done 'well' only when our love of the unseen has 'central' place.[126] As part of the 'organism' through which Christ 'continues to live' in the world, God teaches us how to participate, like children 'taught' by a loving parent.[127] Cooperation also involves God's purifying action, making us 'sharp', 'bright' tools through an 'incessant war' on our 'possessive, narrow intensity', but collaborating in Christ's redeeming work also involves sharing in pain – the 'darkness and mystery of the Cross'.[128]

So Evelyn encouraged her retreatants to both prayer and service, to be both dependent on Christ and in co-operation with him; we 'stretch up' to God in adoration and out to our companions in active love.[129] Echoing the Baron's phrase 'caring matters most', Evelyn stated that retreatants needed to 'care' so much for others that they didn't mind if they had to 'suffer' – we can love the 'tiresome' only when adoring prayer is central.[130]

Prayer

Evelyn taught retreatants some additional principles about prayer. First, it's a 'poor thin' notion to think prayer is something we do 'ourselves', for God takes the initiative, 'teaching' us.[131] Prayer is our 'response' to God, beginning in the will, and our 'attitude' towards God is what's 'most important'.[132] Also, prayer is our *whole life of communion* with God, so there shouldn't be any separation between our devotion and action but rather a 'continuous inner' prayer life.[133] So prayer involves 'every bit of work done toward God', and we need to 'train' ourselves to focus our 'attention' on him through 'fixed times' of prayer to build this 'constant state' of being in his presence.[134]

Aware that we are 'half animal', Evelyn emphasized the role of the body in prayer; our emotions are 'closely connected' with gestures such as kneeling to sustain a 'prayerful mood'.[135] Similarly, our 'spiritual dryness' can be due to 'fatigue' or 'excessive devotional fervour'. When dry, Evelyn suggested retreatants turn to non-religious interests while the 'clouds roll by', and, like the Baron, Evelyn discouraged intensity and strain.[136]

She also helped retreatants deal with distractions in prayer, suggesting that they pray with company early on, or make their 'cares' and 'interests' the subject matter for prayer.[137] She also advocated 'vocal prayers', training us into a continual sense of God's presence, and emphasized that 'lowliness', 'childlikeness' and 'love of neighbour' are proof of our 'union'.[138]

Comparing the spiritual life to gardening, Evelyn stressed our acceptance of whatever prayer God gives us. Rather than weeding 'furiously', leaving 'half of the stems in the ground', we should 'drop' to our 'knees . . . careful not to disturb the growth of the soul in which God has sown His seeds', for God decides what 'sort of garden' it will be. As contemplatives, we may want 'fragile and beautiful flowers', but it may 'suit Him better' to plant in us 'potatoes'.[139]

Spiritual reading

Evelyn taught her retreatants to engage in devotional reading as the 'jewel of devotion', to help 'quiet' their minds.[140] Viewing it as second only to prayer in supporting the inner life, she described it as 'savouring', prayerfully chewing and digesting Scripture and writings from the great souls of the past.[141] Spiritual reading supports adoring prayer as we read his 'great lovers', who were 'masters of adoration', and thus Evelyn recommended the Baron's daily fare: Thomas à Kempis's *Imitation of Christ* and Augustine's *Confessions*.[142] Scripture was also endorsed: 'meditation' on the Gospels 'nourishes' the soul and Psalm reading was repeatedly encouraged; Evelyn even paused at times during her addresses to read a Psalm.[143] As liturgy can bring us into the 'atmosphere of eternity', Evelyn recommended using short 'phrases of adoring love' and Psalm 'fragments' throughout the day.[144]

The three elements

Evelyn emphasized that Bonaventura's three types of prayer – as 'intercessor . . . theologian . . . contemplative' – are all needed for a 'complete' spiritual life but warned of the pitfalls of each: the intellectual element can make prayer too 'thin, abstract and inhuman' and needs balancing with the 'historic' – some 'sacramental integration of spirit and of sense' – while contemplatives can drift into 'quietism' without 'liturgic prayer'; also, Christocentric devotion maintains depth and awe.[145] When praying, we must find the 'form' that 'suits *us*', that God 'shows' us, being aware that as our souls mature our prayer also changes.[146] As we're not all 'nourished' in the same way, we should work out what best 'expands' and 'harmonizes' others, learning about prayer types different to our own.[147]

Slow spiritual formation

Evelyn rebuked our 'spiritual impatience' and 'uppish hurry', seeing Christ's life as our model – thirty years to grow and a few years to act.[148] She emphasized God's 'gradual' action as he 'fosters' and 'sanctifies' growth: no 'shooting up' in a hurry, thus we should not 'strain' but accept what comes, without comparing ourselves to others.[149] And there is to be no 'spiritual gluttony' or 'spiritual ambition', which both spring from 'fussy envy' and 'copy-cat holiness', but instead 'gentle' and 'almost imperceptible' growth, according to God's 'pace'.[150] So, as we help others grow, we must 'feed', not 'force' or 'strain', as well as not hurry, exercising just 'quiet, humble patience', learning the 'artist's pace'.[151] Retreatants should not look too far ahead or wonder where their growth might end but simply respond 'bit by bit', for growth doesn't 'conform' to a 'pattern' and we can't gaze at Christ when we are 'anxious' to get to the 'next stage'.[152]

One essential goal is growing up to the fullness of Christ's 'stature: to put on Christ'.[153] Union with God involves our human nature 'transfigured in Christ', woven into his life and action, absorbing all of who we are to his 'redeeming purpose'.[154] The only way to know the 'cost' is 'contemplation' on Christ's life, losing our own lives through finding his life 'conformed to the Cross', then everything 'falls into place'.[155] For Christ weaves together God's 'life-giving mystery' and 'homeliness' and God works 'on' us, purifying and expanding, but also 'through' us, as we 'touch and modify' others' lives – our souls are 'enlarged'; as we work 'for and with Him . . . we grow'.[156]

Humility

A recurring emphasis in Evelyn's work was the necessity for 'humble self-abandonment', as only those with a 'humble childlike' reception of God are given the 'power' to teach.[157] Evelyn critiqued the 'neglect' of humble duty and joy, which results in a 'lack' of 'spiritual depth and power' in teachers who may be tempted to be popular or superior but end up 'self-poisoned' through pride and self-love.[158] The humbling lesson of our great frailty cures 'cocksureness', and Christ will heal such 'spiritual insomnia' and 'chronic indigestion' through his 'preventative medicine'.[159] Evelyn described love and humility as 'sisters', for as we learn about love we seem to get smaller and God's wonder gets greater; we enter into God's 'very life' through 'self-forgetfulness'.[160]

Suffering

Courage and suffering were viewed as marks of the soul's supernatural life, thus suffering needs to be 'embraced' and 'accepted'.[161] We need to allow God's 'moulding' action to work on our souls, whether or not we 'see the point', for the 'secret of sanctity' is 'humble correspondence' with God in 'whatever He asks' us to do.[162] Joy is the mysterious result of such complete surrender and death to self, and we find peace as we praise God whatever the 'spiritual weather', 'merging' ourselves with his will.[163]

The communion of saints

The fellowship of the saints was repeatedly emphasized by Evelyn. They are God's 'intimate friends', 'examples' to look up to and members of Christ's mystical body. Evelyn even highlighted examples of supernatural heroism and love 'wherever found', emphasizing that we are 'literally members one of another' and that physical death makes 'no difference'.[164] The spirit of the saints sets our spirits on fire, curing our general 'fed-upness'.[165] They are the 'Cloud of Witnesses' we should befriend, as the invisible and visible Church is simply all Christians 'woven into one Body'.[166] Evelyn called retreatants into the support of the saints, joining that 'vast, invisible society, ceaselessly loving and praising God'.[167]

Identity statements and questions

Rather than focus on feelings or consolations – the 'chocolate creams' of the Christian life – retreatants were encouraged into a deepening Christian identity: 'I come from God . . . belong to God . . . am destined for God'; 'I am a child of God . . . a member of Christ, part of a redeemed community'.[168] Evelyn repeatedly encouraged retreatants to view themselves as God's children and 'inheritors of heaven', with one directee told to murmur those words as she drifted to sleep.[169] Retreatants were also asked to ponder the questions: 'What am I for?', 'How am I doing that for which I was born?', 'Do I set any secret limits to the invasion of His grace?', 'What does He want *to do* through me next?'[170]

Deepening clergy

In addition to spiritual retreats, Evelyn was involved in the spiritual formation of Anglican clergy. In 1927 she served on a commission for deepening the spiritual lives of clergy and laity, then around

1930, she wrote *The Way of Renewal* as a memorandum for bishops at Lambeth.[171] She argued that cultivating the 'personal life of prayer' of clergy and nurturing the 'soul' (not just the intellect) were essential for 'spiritual renewal' in the Anglican Church, for the laity need spiritual help, yet seldom receive 'first-hand knowledge of interior ways', which comes only from a 'disciplined' life of prayer. Evelyn argued that in public worship priests often 'fail to evoke the spirit of adoration' as they don't 'possess it themselves', for 'divine renewal' can come only through people of deep prayer. Evelyn recommended that bishops emphasize 'devotional training' in theological colleges and that clergy adopt a 'rule of life' with a 'fixed daily period' of mental prayer and spiritual reading, together with an annual retreat.[172]

Coda

Those who attended Evelyn's retreats provide us with first-hand insights into their value. Lucy Menzies described how Evelyn's flock breathed 'different air' on retreats and were sent back to their jobs 'strengthened, steadied' and 'cheered'.[173] Another retreatant described Evelyn as a 'gateway' to God: having looked so long with adoration and humility on the things of eternity, she 'reflected' that 'vision' to her retreatants.[174] Cropper identified Evelyn's greatest 'gift' in leading retreats as her 'sense of God'; the 'overagainstness' that the Baron had 'commended' to her, came through to her hearers with 'overwhelming' but 'peaceful insistence'.[175]

Retreat leading and spiritual direction became key avenues for Evelyn to provide spiritual formation. As she aged she gave fewer retreats but continued giving spiritual direction. And she began to look forward to heaven, imagining it as both 'absolutely happy and absolutely dark, to protect us from the blaze of God'.[176]

We close with one of Evelyn's favourite prayers recited at all her retreats:

Defend and keep the souls of Your little servants among so many perils of this corruptible life, and Your Grace going with us, direct us by the way of peace to the country of everlasting clearness.[177]

Afterword

Though I never had the privilege of personally meeting Evelyn Underhill or Friedrich von Hügel, I did get to know Eugene Peterson as my teacher at Regent College Vancouver (1995–8) and through letter writing thereafter. I still vividly recall the first time I heard Eugene's *raspy* voice speaking at the front of Chapel. Alongside his refreshing sense of humour and careful, poetic use of language, I soon came to recognize that Eugene had really good instincts regarding theology and formation, from having immersed himself prayerfully in Scripture for decades. I quote Eugene endlessly when teaching students and leading retreats – both from my memories of what he said (and who he was – his kindness and humility) and from his writings. It was Eugene who taught me about praying the Psalms and Sabbath-keeping. Through his influence I found myself praying, 'What are you doing, God, and how can I participate?' – which has been a prayer for me for over two decades. I didn't know at the time that Eugene had gained this sense of the prevenience of God from the Baron. Eugene helped to usher me into an expectancy that God initiates and sets things up and we simply participate in *his* work. And it was through Eugene that I was introduced to the Baron.

Eugene Peterson described von Hügel as his 'most formative' guide, the 'wisest' of 'masters' and a 'significant voice' he had engaged in 'prayerful conversation with' over several decades.[1] The Quaker Douglas Steere introduced Eugene to the Baron on a silent retreat; thereafter Eugene attributed the Baron's 'shaping influence' on him as 'second only' in matters of 'maturity' to St Paul in Ephesians.[2] Eugene viewed the Baron as one of the 'giants' in the land, who was yet on the whole 'ignored' by Protestants (particularly evangelicals), and he couldn't work out why the Baron hadn't made it into the 'spirituality canon', for here was a 'mature man who knew what it meant to measure up to the 'full stature of Christ'.[3]

Eugene found the Baron the most 'sane, balanced and wise mind/spirit' of his acquaintance; someone who had absorbed the 'deeply lived truth' of the centuries and cared about living the Christian faith 'well', not just 'talking' or 'arguing' about it.[4] In terms of formation, Eugene said that it was primarily the Baron's 'attention to souls' in his letters that 'influenced' him, for the Baron dealt with 'persons and particulars', not the 'depersonalized' unloading of 'abstract' advice.[5] Eugene was reminded that every soul is 'unique' and cannot be encouraged, understood or 'directed' through 'general' advice or a 'superficial diagnosis using psychological categories'. He came to recognize the value of letter-writing in formation, and was astonished that no one had focused on the 'main thing' the Baron did – 'spiritual direction'![6]

Eugene was critical of the state of spiritual direction today, with so much shaped by 'Jungian psychology' and a kind of 'therapeutic counselling sprinkled with holy water'.[7] Hence the necessity to dig 'deeper' under the spiritual direction 'faddishness' by tapping into someone who didn't 'understand' himself as a 'spiritual director' but simply placed himself, 'unconsciously', into an 'attentive and praying presence with another'.[8]

In *The Pastor* (2011), Eugene described the Baron as 'conspicuous' for his sheer 'sanity' of direction as he sorted out people's lives in matters of 'love', 'faith and obedience'. But as he continued to read the Baron's letters, he realized they were addressed to him, as a pastor 'searching for a language and disposition for discerning a whole and healthy way of life'. The Baron's letters were 'forming' him in a 'pastoral' way through conversational language:[9]

> not condescending, not manipulative, but attentive and prayerful. Not instructional . . . Not diagnostic, treating these unique souls as problems to be fixed . . . as I read and reread

and reread, I was letting von Hügel soak me in holy mysteries, so that as I talked and listened informally, conversationally, without pastoral self-consciousness, I was inviting people into the ways of God that are 'past understanding', not just instructing them in how to get across the street without stepping into moral mud puddles. I recognized this as holy wisdom, knowledge distilled into reflexes and synapses, knowledge lived. I needed to keep company with this man . . . I didn't want to be a pastor who treated souls as dittos.[10]

Eugene found in the Baron a writer who 'confirmed' for him what is involved in 'growing up in Christ' and who over many years was a 'faithful companion' in the 'practice of resurrection'.[11] The Baron helped Eugene understand the 'formation' of our minds, spirits and souls – 'our lives transformed . . . growing to maturity, to the stature of Christ'.[12]

Evelyn Underhill wrote that the 'full number' of the Baron's 'spiritual children will never be known', nor the 'extent' to which his 'advice, teaching and support' came to 'fertilize the most distant corners of the Christian field'.[13] Eugene Peterson is a case in point, as he indicated that the Baron is 'present (usually unquoted) on most pages' of *Practice Resurrection* (2010) and many of his thirty other books.[14] Like Evelyn, Eugene communicated the Baron's insights to a broader audience than the Baron could reach himself – 'One torch lights another.'

We close with the words of Gwendolen Greene, the person most nurtured by the Baron:

[The Baron] lived in a deep interior world where few, perhaps, can follow – giving himself to an interior life; tearing, as it were, out of himself great chunks of truth and bringing them to the surface, explaining to us what we can gather and understand.[15]

Notes

Foreword

1 Von Hügel, *Selected*, 266.

2 Von Hügel, *Selected*, 38.

3 Von Hügel, *Selected*, 137.

4 Von Hügel, *Selected*, 147.

Chapter 1

1 G. Greene (ed.), *Niece*, viii–ix.

2 Armstrong, *Evelyn*, 236.

3 Williams (ed.), *Letters*, 196.

4 Bodleian Library, MSS Eng. Misc. d. 1117, fol. 34.

5 William Inge, in Steere, *Together*, 42.

6 Charles Gore, cited in de la Bédoyère, *Life*, xi.

7 Steere, *Counsels*, 5.

8 De la Bédoyère, *Life*, 20.

9 Georgetown University Special Collections, de la Bédoyère Papers, Box 1, Folder 2.

10 Von Hügel, *Essays II*, 255; *German*, 123.

11 Holland (ed.), *Selected*, 334.

12 Gibbard, 'Friedrich', 13.

13 Bodleian Library, MSS Eng. Misc. d. 1117, fol. 34; SAUL, MS 37184/47a.

14 Von Hügel, *Reality*, 28–9, 37.

15 Holland (ed.), *Selected*, 4.

16 Von Hügel, 'Apologist', 860.

17 Von Hügel, *Reality*, 27.

18 De la Bédoyère, *Life*, 191–2.

19 DAA, MS 3570. VII. A. 3. f.

20 Holland (ed.), *Selected*, 255–6.

21 D'Arcy, *Laughter*, 79–80.

22 Von Hügel, *Reality*, 80.

23 Von Hügel, *Reality*, 79–80, 81.

24 Von Hügel, *Reality*, 95.

25 Von Hügel, *Essays II*, 98–9.

26 Von Hügel, *Essays II*, 97.

27 Von Hügel, *Essays II*, 98.

28 De la Bédoyère, *Life*, 18.

29 SAUL, MS 38776/8.

30 Steere, *Together*, 43–4; G. Greene (ed.), *Niece*, xxiv.

31 G. Greene (ed.), *Niece*, 85–6.

32 De la Bédoyère, *Life*, 23.

33 Butler, 'Friedrich', 184; Holland, 'Memoir'; Holland, *Selected*, 49.

34 G. Greene (ed.), *Niece*, 45, xxxii, 130.

35 Von Hügel, *Reality*, 22.

36 British Museum, Petre Papers, Letter from von Hügel to Maude Petre, 15–16 December 1910.

37 G. Greene (ed.), *Niece*, xv; von Hügel, *Essays I*, 286.

38 G. Greene (ed.), *Niece*, 75.

39 Von Hügel, 'Louis', 342.

40 De la Bédoyère, *Life*, 42–3; von Hügel, *Essays I*, 286; von Hügel, *Mystical* (1923), 1: vii; G. Greene (ed.), *Niece*, xxiv.

41 Louis-Lefebvre, *Abbé*, 167.

42 Huvelin, *Guides*, xlii; Huvelin, *Addresses*, 47; SAUL, MS 2694.

43 Von Hügel, 'Spiritual', 991.

44 Von Hügel, *Eternal*, 375–6.

45 Underhill, *Supernatural*, 256.

46 Barmann, 'Baron', 64.

47 Von Hügel, *Selected*, 248.

48 Campbell, *New*, 33.

49 Lillie, *Some*, 2.

50 Von Hügel, *Reality*, 32; G. Greene (ed.), *Niece*, xxxvi.

51 Von Hügel, *Essays II*, 121.

52 Steere, *Counsels*, 5.

53 Von Hügel, *Reality*, 6.

54 De la Bédoyère, *Life*, 328, 71.

55 Barmann (ed.), *Letters*, 156.

56 Underhill, *Mixed*, 233.

57 SAUL, von Hügel's diary, 20 March 1918; 11 May 1919; 6 March 1919.

58 Garceau, *Little*, 286.

59 Beattie, 'Sense', 43.

60 Von Hügel, *Mystical* (1908), 1: vi.

61 Steere, *Doors*, 169.

62 Holland (ed.), *Selected*, 102–3; de la Bédoyère, *Life*, xi.

63 Edinburgh University Library Special Collections, GB 237 Coll 1038.

64 Von Hügel, *Reality*, 3.

65 Holland (ed.), *Selected*, 190.

66 See Kelly, *Baron*, 18–24.

67 Lester-Garland, *Religious*, 7–8; Barmann (ed.), *Letters*, 66.

68 Lester-Garland, *Religious*, 7–8.

69 Kemp Smith in Barmann (ed.), *Letters*, 145.

70 Petre, *Way*, 78.

71 Lillie, *Some*, 6–7.

72 Barmann (ed.), *Letters*, 256.

73 De la Bédoyère, *Life*, 9.

74 Shulbred Priory Archive, Arthur Ponsonby's Diaries, n.d.; Hubert Parry Diaries, October–November 1893, 168–9.

75 De la Bédoyère, *Life*, 9.

76 Mansel, 'Letter', 2.

77 De la Bédoyère, *Life*, 270.

78 SAUL, von Hügel's diary, 18 October 1922.

79 De la Bédoyère, *Life*, 53.

80 Holland (ed.), *Selected*, 66, 54.

81 Nottinghill Carmelite Priory Archive, Letter from Sr Thekla von Hügel to Sr Mary Assumpta, July 1963.

82 Ward, *Insurrection*, 507–8.

83 De la Bédoyère, *Life*, 288–9.

84 G. Greene (ed.), *Niece*, 123.

85 Mansel, 'Letter', 1.

86 Barrows, *Frances*, 123.

87 De la Bédoyère, *Life*, 86.

88 Holland (ed.), *Selected*, 374.

89 Bodleian Library, MSS Eng. Misc. d. 1117, fols. 34–35.

90 Ward, *Insurrection*, 161; Barmann (ed.), *Letters*, 219.

91 SAUL, MS 30628.

92 Underhill, *Mixed*, 230.

93 Underhill, *Mixed*, 209.

94 Underhill, *Mixed*, 209.

95 Underhill, *Mixed*, 233, 230.

96 Underhill, *Mixed*, 210.

97 Underhill, *Mixed*, 209, 210.

98 Underhill, *Mixed*, 299.

99 Underhill, *Mixed*, 232.

100 Underhill, *Mixed*, 233.

101 Holland (ed.), *Selected*, 55.

102 Holland (ed.), *Selected*, 55–6.

103 Ward, *Insurrection*, 513.

104 D'Arcy, *Laughter*, 79.

105 De la Bédoyère, *Life*, 151.

106 D'Arcy, *Laughter*, 80.

107 SAUL, MS 3069.

108 Quoted in Holland, 'Memoir', 53; Misner, *Friedrich*, 53.

109 Petre, *Way*, 255; BL, Add. MS 52376; Petre, *Tyrrell*, 6.

110 Ward, *Insurrection*, 514–15.

111 Steuart, *Diversity*, 152–3; Psalm 75:25.

Chapter 2

1 G. Greene (ed.), *Niece*, xv.

2 PA, Lucy Menzies, Unpublished MS; Cropper, *Life*; Armstrong, *Evelyn*; D. Greene, *Artist*.

3 PA, Armstrong Box, Letter from E. I. Watkin to Fr Dom Daniel, 17 July 1976.

4 PA, Menzies, Unpublished MS, VI.9.

5 Poston (ed.), *Making*, 13.

6 KCLA, K/PP75, 3/3/1.

7 Williams (ed.), *Letters*, 125, 122.

8 Armstrong, *Evelyn*, 8.

9 Armstrong, *Evelyn*, 8–9, 18.

10 Armstrong, *Evelyn*, 10.

11 Armstrong, *Evelyn*, 11; Williams (ed.), *Letters*, 11.

12 Williams (ed.), *Letters*, 125.

13 Cropper, *Life*, 13.

14 Williams (ed.), *Letters*, 12.

15 PA, Menzies, Unpublished MS, III.11; D. Greene, *Artist*, 13.

16 PA, Menzies, Unpublished MS, II.19.

17 Underhill, 'Cant', 755.

18 Armstrong, *Evelyn*, 37–8.

19 Armstrong, *Evelyn*, 36.

20 Armstrong, *Evelyn*, 38.

21 Underhill, 'Magic', 764–5.

22 Williams (ed.), *Letters*, 125.

23 Williams (ed.), *Letters*, 125–6.

24 Cropper, *Life*, 29.

25 KCLA, K/PP75, 1/2/7, 8 April 1907.

26 KCLA, K/PP75, 3/3/2; 3/3/3; 3/3/4.

27 Williams (ed.), *Letters*, 126; Armstrong, *Evelyn*, 57.

28 KCLA, K/PP75, 1/2/15.

29 Cropper, *Life*, 31; Armstrong, *Evelyn*, 56.

30 Armstrong, *Evelyn*, 57.

31 Williams (ed.), *Letters*, 126, 77.

32 Cropper, *Life*, 42.

33 Cropper, *Life*, 229.

34 Cropper, *Life*, 34; PA, Menzies, Unpublished MS, VI.9.

35 PA, Menzies, Unpublished MS, VI.9.

36 D. Green, *Artist*, 36.

37 PA, Menzies, Unpublished MS, VI.11.

38 Cropper, *Life*, 32; D. Greene, *Artist*, 35.

39 Cropper, *Life*, 251.

40 Cropper, *Life*, 230.

41 Cropper, *Life*, 248.

42 Armstrong, *Evelyn*, 161.

43 Cropper, *Life*, 196.

44 PA, Menzies, Unpublished MS, VIII.2.

45 Williams (ed.), *Letters*, 128; D. Greene, *Artist*, 35.

46 Steere, *Gleanings*, 58.

47 Williams (ed.), *Letters*, 83, 180, 158.

48 Williams (ed.), *Letters*, 102, 232.

49 Williams (ed.), *Letters*, 214; PA, Menzies, Unpublished MS, VIII.1.

50 Cropper, *Life*, 247.

51 Poston (ed.), *Making*, 152.

52 PA, Menzies, Unpublished MS, VI.11; V.1.

53 Armstrong, *Evelyn*, 96.

54 PA, Menzies, Unpublished MS, VI.11.

55 PA, Menzies, Unpublished MS, XI, VIII, XI.

56 D. Greene (ed.), *Fragments*, 18; Allchin, *Kingdom*, 185.

57 Williams (ed.), *Letters*, 107.

58 SAUL, Hug B828.U7.

59 SAUL, von Hügel's diary, 16 July 1911.

60 Armstrong, *Evelyn*, 131; Underhill, *Mysticism*, xxi.

61 Armstrong, *Evelyn*, 132.

62 Underhill, *Mysticism*, xvi.

63 Williams (ed.), *Letters*, 129.

64 Holland (ed.), *Selected*, 187.

65 D. Greene, *Artist*, 40.

66 SAUL, von Hügel's diary, 10 and 11 December 1912.

67 SAUL, Hug B828.U6.

68 Cropper, *Life*, 52.

69 Williams (ed.), *Letters*, 141.

70 Williams (ed.), *Letters*, 144.

71 Williams (ed.), *Letters*, 144; Poston (ed.), *Making*, 244.

72 KCLA, K/PP75, Obituaries, 9/2, 18 June 1941.

73 Armstrong, *Evelyn*, 155.

74 PA, Menzies, Unpublished MS, VI.14.

75 Underhill, *Immanence*, 1.

76 Williams (ed.), *Letters*, 144; KCLA, K/PP75, Folder 31, 1/20/11.

77 Wrigley-Carr (ed.), *Evelyn*, 35.

78 SAUL, Hug BV5081.U6; Armstrong, *Evelyn*, 190.

79 Armstrong, *Evelyn*, 160.

80 PA, Menzies, Unpublished MS, VI.13.

81 Underhill, 'Modern', 234–8.

82 KCLA, K/PP75, 1/10/1.

83 KCLA, K/PP75, 1/10/1, 26 June 1916.

84 KCLA, K/PP75, 1/10/3, 14 December 1916.

85 A. Underhill, *Change*, 105; PA, Menzies, Unpublished MS, XI.

86 SAUL, MS 5552.

87 Williams (ed.), *Letters*, 147–8.

88 SAUL, MS 5552; D. Greene (ed.), *Fragments*, 20.

89 Underhill, 'Future', 336.

90 D. Greene (ed.), *Guide*, 66.

91 SAUL, Hug B828.U7E8.

92 Underhill, *Mixed*, 230; Williams (ed.), *Letters*, 170.

93 G. Greene (ed.), *Niece*, 174.

94 KCLA, K/PP75, 3/3/1.

95 KCLA, K/PP75, 3/3/1; G. Greene (ed.), *Niece*, 174.

96 G. Greene (ed.), *Niece*, 174.

97 KCLA, K/PP75, 3/3/1.

98 SAUL, MS 5552.

99 Cropper, *Life*, 70.

100 G. Greene (ed.), *Niece*, 174.

101 Armstrong, *Evelyn*, 136.

102 KCLA, K/PP75, 3/3/1.

103 G. Greene (ed.), *Niece*, 174–5.

104 PA, Menzies, Unpublished MS, IX.21.

105 SAUL, von Hügel's diary, 22 July 1922; 6 July 1922.

106 SAUL, von Hügel's diary, 17 April 1924; 5 May 1924; 29 May 1924.

107 G. Greene (ed.), *Niece*, 174–5.

108 Cropper, *Life*, 85.

109 Cropper, *Life*, 89.

110 Cropper, *Life*, 69.

111 Underhill, *Spirit*, xvii–xviii; SAUL, Hug BV5082.U6.

112 Armstrong, *Evelyn*, 190.

113 SAUL, Hug BV5080.H5.

114 SAUL, MS 38494/1.

115 PA, Menzies, Unpublished MS, X.4.

116 Armstrong, *Evelyn*, 205; D. Greene (ed.), *Fragments*, 27.

117 Allchin, *Kingdom*, 187.

118 Underhill, *Spirit*, 147.

119 Cropper, *Life*, 96.

120 D. Greene (ed.), *Fragments*, 40.

121 D. Greene (ed.), *Fragments*, 35, 55–6.

122 D. Greene (ed.), *Fragments*, 65.

123 D. Greene (ed.), *Fragments*, 57–8.

124 D. Greene (ed.), *Fragments*, 58, 60, 65.

125 D. Greene (ed.), *Fragments*, 60, 48, 62.

126 Armstrong, *Evelyn*, 234, 235.

127 Armstrong, *Evelyn*, 235.

128 Williams (ed.), *Letters*, 28.

129 Williams (ed.), *Letters*, 162.

130 KCLA, K/PP75, 1/21/1.

131 Cropper, *Life*, 141, 147.

132 Cropper, *Life*, 198, 141.

133 Cropper, *Life*, 158–9.

134 Cropper, *Life*, 143; Poston (ed.), *Making*, 239.

135 Underhill, *Supernatural*, ix.

136 Williams (ed.), *Letters*, 177.

137 D. Greene (ed.), *Fragments*, 75; KCLA, K/PP75, 1/27/12.

138 Armstrong, *Evelyn*, 246.

139 Armstrong, *Evelyn*, 247.

140 D. Greene (ed.), *Fragments*, 78; Cropper, *Life*, 163.

141 Armstrong, *Evelyn*, 248.

142 Cropper, *Life*, 164.

143 Williams (ed.), *Letters*, 36.

144 Cropper, *Life*, 162; Poston (ed.), *Making*, 249.

145 Chapman, *Spiritual*, 106.

146 Williams (ed.), *Letters*, 220, 244, 245.

147 D. Greene (ed.), *Fragments*, 88–9.

148 KCLA, K/PP75, 1/27/28; Poston (ed.), *Making*, 313, 327.

149 Community of the Resurrection, Mirfield, Archive, Letter from Edward Talbot to an ex-pupil, 1897.

150 D. Greene (ed.), *Fragments*, 90.

151 Armstrong, *Evelyn*, 251.

152 Armstrong, *Evelyn*, 252.

153 Cropper, *Life*, 241.

154 Cropper, *Life*, 174.

155 Cropper, *Life*, 183.

156 Goodacre, 'Ward', 389.

157 Morgan, *Reginald*, 21, 27.

158 D. Greene (ed.), *Fragments*, 93.

159 D. Greene (ed.), *Fragments*, 94.

160 D. Greene (ed.), *Fragments*, 95.

161 Poston (ed.), *Making*, 270; KCLA, K/PP75, 1/27/28.

162 D. Greene (ed.), *Fragments*, 97.

163 D. Greene (ed.), *Fragments*, 98.

164 D. Greene (ed.), *Fragments*, 99.

165 D. Greene (ed.), *Fragments*, 100.

166 Goodacre, 'Ward', 390; Armstrong, *Evelyn*, 252.

167 Morgan, *Reginald*, 81, 104–5, 40.

168 D. Greene (ed.), *Fragments*, 101.

169 Armstrong, *Evelyn*, 253.

170 Williams (ed.), *Letters*, 204–5.

171 Cropper, *Life*, 139; Williams (ed.), *Letters*, 160.

172 Cropper, *Life*, 139.

173 KCLA, K/PP75, 1/13/9.

174 KCLA, K/PP75, 1/13/4; 1/13/14; 1/13/15.

175 KCLA, K/PP75, 1/13/16.

176 KCLA, K/PP75, 1/13/23; 1/13/26.

177 Holland (ed.), *Selected*, 60.

178 Williams (ed.), *Letters*, 207, 152.

179 Williams (ed.), *Letters*, 209.

180 Williams (ed.), *Letters*, 151.

181 Williams (ed.), *Letters*, 126.

182 Williams (ed.), *Letters*, 207–8; PA, Menzies, Unpublished MS, VI.15.

183 Williams (ed.), *Letters*, 211; Allchin, *Kingdom*, 188.

184 Williams (ed.), *Letters*, 126.

185 Williams (ed.), *Letters*, 195–6.

186 Williams (ed.), *Letters*, 210.

187 Armstrong, *Evelyn*, xii.

188 Williams (ed.), *Letters*, 267; Allchin, *Kingdom*, 193.

189 Underhill, *Eastern*, 13.

190 Underhill, *Worship*, xii.

191 Armstrong, *Evelyn*, 279.

192 PA, Menzies, Unpublished MS, VIII.8.

193 PA, Menzies, Unpublished MS, VIII.8.

194 Williams (ed.), *Letters*, 256–7; Underhill, *Light*, 107.

195 Cropper, *Life*, 154.

196 Underhill, *Light*, 41.

197 Armstrong, *Evelyn*, 288; Underhill, 'War', 215.

198 Cropper, *Life*, 224–5; Williams (ed.), *Letters*, 305; Cropper, *Life*, 228.

199 Williams (ed.), *Letters*, 308.

200 Underhill, 'Postscript', in D. Greene (ed.), *Guide*, 208; Cropper, *Life*, 242; Underhill, *Fruits*, 56, 50.

201 Underhill, 'Postscript', in D. Greene (ed.), *Guide*, 206.

202 D. Greene (ed.), *Guide*, 202; Underhill, 'Postscript', in D. Greene (ed.), *Guide*, 207; Underhill, 'War', 213–14.

203 Underhill, 'War', 216; Underhill, 'Postscript', in D. Greene (ed.), *Guide*, 205.

204 Underhill, *Peace*, NP.

205 Steere, *Gleanings*, 56.

206 Armstrong, *Evelyn*, 241.

207 PA, Menzies, Unpublished MS, IV.6.

208 Cropper, *Life*, 223.

209 Cropper, *Life*, 216.

210 Cropper, *Life*, 237.

211 Cropper, *Life*, 233.

212 Poston (ed.), *Making*, 318; Cropper, *Life*, 218.

213 Armstrong, *Evelyn*, 291.

214 KCLA, K/PP75, 8/4.

215 KCLA, K/PP75, 8/4.

216 Cropper, *Life*, 195–6.

217 Ramsay, 'Foreword', in Armstrong, *Evelyn*, x.

Chapter 3

1 Underhill, *Mixed*, 233.

2 Williams (ed.), *Letters*, 196.

3 Williams (ed.), *Letters*, 196.

4 Menzies, 'Memoir', 20; Williams (ed.), *Letters*, 319.

5 Von Hügel, *Mystical* (1908), 1: 70.

6 Underhill, *Mixed*, 215.

7 De la Bédoyère, *Life*, 113; Holland (ed.), *Selected*, 201.

8 Von Hügel, *Essays I*, 278.

9 Holland (ed.), *Selected*, 95.

10 Underhill, *Mixed*, 213.

11 Von Hügel, *Essays I*, 254.

12 G. Greene (ed.), *Niece*, 69, xxxviii.

13 G. Greene (ed.), *Niece*, xxxvi, 95.

14 Barmann (ed.), *Letters*, 37.

15 Von Hügel, *Eternal*, 323–4.

16 G. Greene (ed.), *Niece*, xxxvii.

17 SAUL, MS 5552/1.

18 SAUL, MS 5552/55.

19 SAUL, MS 5552/3.

20 Steere, *Dimensions*, 115.

21 Williams (ed.), *Letters*, 207, 238.

22 G. Greene (ed.), *Niece*, xxv.

23 SAUL, MS 37194/6b.

24 Holland (ed.), *Selected*, 209.

25 Von Hügel, *Eternal*, 370; Holland (ed.), *Selected*, 216.

26 SAUL, MS 38776/8; MS 37194/6b; G. Greene (ed.), *Niece*, xxv.

27 Von Hügel, *Reality*, 144.

28 Von Hügel, *Eternal*, 86; von Hügel, *Mystical* (1908), 1: 59.

29 Von Hügel, *Reality*, 144; Lillie, *Some*, 40.

30 G. Greene (ed.), *Niece*, 47.

31 Mansel, 'Letter', 3.

32 Cropper, *Life*, 112; KCLA, K/PP75, 3/3/1.

33 Holland (ed.), *Selected*, 326.

34 G. Greene (ed.), *Niece*, xxxiii.

35 G. Greene (ed.), *Niece*, xxxiv, xxxi.

36 Holland (ed.), *Selected*, 220.

37 G. Greene, 'Baron', 131.

38 Williams (ed.), *Letters*, 216; Underhill, *Mixed*, 210.

39 Armstrong, *Life*, 212.

40 Underhill, *Mixed*, 212.

41 Steere, *Dimensions*, 41–2.

42 Holland (ed.), *Selected*, 252–3.

43 Steere, *Dimensions*, 123.

44 Von Hügel, *Reality*, 32.

45 Holland (ed.), *Selected*, 320.

46 Holland (ed.), *Selected*, 319–20.

47 Von Hügel, *Eternal*, 329–30.

48 Von Hügel, *Eternal*, 325.

49 SAUL, MS 5552/39.

50 Kelly, 'Friend', 79.

51 Petre, *Way*, 222.

52 Kelly, 'Friend', 79; Barmann (ed.), *Letters*, 125.

53 G. Greene (ed.), *Niece*, 187; von Hügel, *Reality*, 148.

54 SAUL, MS 5552/1; Cropper, *Life*, 97.

55 Cropper, *Life*, 118–19.

56 Mansel, 'Letter', 7; Cropper, *Life*, 114.

57 G. Greene, *Two*, 127.

58 G. Greene (ed.), *Niece*, xlii–iii.

59 G. Greene, *Two*, 127; KCLA, K/PP75, 3/3/1.

60 G. Greene (ed.), *Niece*, xxxiii; von Hügel, *Mystical* (1908), 2: 126; von Hügel, *Essays II*, 228.

61 Von Hügel, *Eternal*, 332; von Hügel, *Reality*, 32.

62 Cropper, *Life*, 113.

63 Cropper, *Life*, 113; SAUL, MS 5552.

64 Von Hügel, *Essays II*, 232–3.

65 De la Bédoyère, *Life*, 254.

66 Mansel, 'Letter', 6–7.

67 Mansel, 'Letter', 7.

68 Mansel, 'Letter', 7–8.

69 G. Greene, *Two*, 134.

70 SAUL, MS 5552/57–58.

71 Von Hügel, *Eternal*, 342.

72 Von Hügel, *Eternal*, 342 (emphasis original).

73 De la Bédoyère, *Life*, 165–6.

74 Barmann (ed.), *Letters*, 282.

75 Cropper, *Life*, 99–100; SAUL, MS 5552/39.

76 SAUL, MS 5552/1.

77 Williams (ed.), *Letters*, 234.

78 SAUL, MS 5552/1.

79 G. Greene (ed.), *Niece*, 174; Cropper, *Life*, 74.

80 Cropper, *Life*, 81–2.

81 Cropper, *Life*, 86.

82 Cropper, *Life*, 95–6.

83 SAUL, MS 5552/42–43.

84 KCLA, K/PP75, 3/3/2; 3/3/3; 3/3/4.

85 Cropper, *Life*, 181.

86 D. Greene (ed.), *Fragments*, 80.

87 Poston (ed.), *Making*, 194.

88 Underhill, *Mysticism*, xiv.

89 Barmann, 'Modernist', 221–2.

90 Underhill, *Mixed*, 231–2.

91 Von Hügel, *Reality*, 91.

92 G. Greene (ed.), *Niece*, 147.

93 Lillie, *Some*, 50.

94 G. Greene (ed.), *Niece*, xxix.

95 Community of the Resurrection, Mirfield, Archive, Edward Talbot's Papers; Underhill, *Mixed*, 232.

96 G. Greene (ed.), *Niece*, 14; SAUL, MS 36349/2.

97 G. Greene (ed.), *Niece*, xx, 4.

98 Cropper, *Life*, 78, 98.

99 Cropper, *Life*, 98–9.

100 Cropper, *Life*, 77–8.

101 Williams (ed.), *Letters*, 175–6.

102 Cropper, *Life*, 116.

103 Cropper, *Life*, 111.

104 Cropper, *Life*, 111.

105 Cropper, *Life*, 116, 75.

106 KCLA, K/PP75, 3/3/1.

107 G. Greene (ed.), *Niece*, 46.

108 G. Greene (ed.), *Niece*, 46, xx.

109 Williams (ed.), *Letters*, 264–5.

110 Cropper, *Life*, 77–8.

111 Cropper, *Life*, 99.

112 Underhill, *Mixed*, 231.

113 G. Greene (ed.), *Niece*, xi–xii.

114 Cropper, *Life*, 118.

115 G. Greene (ed.), *Niece*, xlv.

116 Cropper, *Life*, 76.

117 Cropper, *Life*, 90–1.

118 Cropper, *Life*, 91.

119 Underhill, *Mixed*, 231–2.

120 SAUL, MS VII.143.196a.

121 SAUL, MS VII.143.196a–b; Barmann (ed.), *Letters*, 290.

122 G. Greene (ed.), *Niece*, 75;
    SAUL, MS VII.143.196a–b;
    Holland (ed.), *Selected*, 203;
    SAUL, MS 37174/7.

123 SAUL, MS VII.143.196a–b;
    MS 37194/27a; MS
    37194/18a.

124 SAUL, MS VII.143.196a–b.

125 SAUL, MS VII.143.196;
    Mansel, 'Letter', 6.

126 Williams (ed.), *Letters*, 324.

127 Holland (ed.), *Selected*, 341.

128 G. Greene (ed.), *Niece*, 130,
    xxxii.

129 KCLA, K/PP75, 3/3/1.

130 G. Greene (ed.), *Niece*, 37, 43.

131 G. Greene (ed.), *Niece*, xxii;
    Underhill, *Mixed*, 229.

132 G. Greene (ed.), *Niece*, 121, 181.

133 Cropper, *Life*, 89–90, 97.

134 G. Greene (ed.), *Niece*, 198,
    105.

135 Cropper, *Life*, 114.

136 KCLA, K/PP75, 3/3/1.

137 Cropper, *Life*, 90; D. Greene
    (ed.), *Fragments*, 15.

138 Armstrong, *Evelyn*, 210.

139 SAUL, MS BV5095.U6;
    Allchin, *Kingdom*, 194; SAUL,
    MS 5552/37.

140 KCLA, K/PP75, 3/3/2.

141 Williams (ed.), *Letters*, 237;
    Cropper, *Life*, 115–16.

142 Cropper, *Life*, 98.

143 SAUL, MS 5552/57.

144 Cropper, *Life*, 110.

145 SAUL, MS 5552/55.

146 Cropper, *Life*, 101.

147 SAUL, MS 5552/55.

148 Cropper, *Life*, 118.

149 G. Greene (ed.), *Niece*, 62;
    Von Hügel, *Essays II*, 229.

150 Underhill, *Mixed*, 214.

151 SAUL, MS 5552/40–44; MS
    BV5095.U6/32.

152 G. Greene (ed.), *Niece*, xxxii.

153 G. Greene (ed.), *Niece*, 62–3;
    Mansel, 'Letter', 4; University
    of San Francisco Special
    Collections, Modernist
    Collection, Letter from
    von Hügel to E. I. Watkin;
    G. Greene (ed.), *Niece*, 107.

154 G. Greene (ed.), *Niece*, 121.

155 G. Greene, 'Recollections',
    148.

156 Holland (ed.), *Selected*, 94;
    G. Greene (ed.), *Niece*, xxxii.

157 G. Greene (ed.), *Niece*, 179,
    182.

158 G. Greene (ed.), *Niece*, 196;
    Kelly (ed.), *Letters*, 109.

159 Holland (ed.), *Selected*, 156;
    DAA, 3570. IX1271.

160 D. Greene (ed.), *Fragments*,
    54–5.

161 SAUL, MS 5552.

162 Cropper, *Life*, 76; Barmann (ed.), *Letters*, 134.

163 G. Greene (ed.), *Niece*, 111, 109.

164 G. Greene (ed.), *Niece*, 46.

165 G. Greene (ed.), *Niece*, 101, 108.

166 Von Hügel, *Essays II*, 227.

167 G. Greene (ed.), *Niece*, xxii, xxi.

168 G. Greene, 'Recollections', 148.

169 G. Greene (ed.), *Niece*, 108.

170 G. Greene (ed.), *Niece*, xxi.

171 G. Greene (ed.), *Niece*, xl.

172 Huvelin, *Guides*, 37–8, 11; von Hügel, *Eternal*, 375.

173 Huvelin, *Guides*, 15; 'Saying XV', in Holland (ed.), *Selected*, 60; G. Greene, 'Baron', 129.

174 SAUL, MS 38776/9.

175 SAUL, MS 38776/9.

176 Armstrong, *Evelyn*, 212.

177 G. Greene, 'Baron', 130.

178 G. Greene (ed.), *Niece*, 169–70.

179 G. Greene (ed.), *Niece*, 188, 80, 179.

180 SAUL, MS 5552/57; Cropper, *Life*, 76.

181 SAUL, MS 5552/1; Cropper, *Life*, 119.

182 G. Greene (ed.), *Niece*, xx–xxi.

183 SAUL, MS 37194/11/1a; G. Greene (ed.), *Niece*, 93; DAA, MS 3570, IX.1272.

184 Cropper, *Life*, 92.

185 Cropper, *Life*, 98.

186 Nédoncelle, *Baron*, 92–3.

187 G. Greene (ed.), *Niece*, xliii.

188 D. Greene (ed.), *Fragments*, 33; Cropper, *Life*, 147.

189 G. Greene (ed.), *Niece*, 72.

190 Von Hügel, *Eternal*, 69.

191 Von Hügel, *Eternal*, 378, 89.

192 Von Hügel, *Mystical* (1908), 1: 239.

193 Von Hügel, *Eternal*, 382; Augustine, *Writings*, 115.

194 Von Hügel, *Eternal*, 1.

195 Von Hügel, *Eternal*, 372.

196 Von Hügel, *Eternal*, 390.

197 Von Hügel, *Eternal*, 392–3.

198 DAA, MS IX1272.

199 Von Hügel, *Eternal*, 367.

200 Von Hügel, *Eternal*, 317, 316, 123.

201 Von Hügel, *Eternal*, xiii.

202 Von Hügel, *Eternal*, 385.

203 Von Hügel, *Essays I*, 288.

204 Von Hügel, *Eternal*, 368.

205 Von Hügel, *Eternal*, 369.

206 Von Hügel, *Eternal*, 378.

207 G. Greene (ed.), *Niece*, 166–7.

208 Von Hügel, *Essays I*, 99.

209 Von Hügel, *Mystical* (1923), 1: xix.

210 Von Hügel, *Essays II*, 223.

211 Von Hügel, *Essays II*, 224.

212 G. Greene (ed.), *Niece*, xxviii, xviii.

213 Underhill, *Mixed*, 233; SAUL, MS 37194/29.

214 Holland (ed.), *Selected*, 88.

215 G. Greene (ed.), *Niece*, 118.

216 Cropper, *Life*, 75.

217 Williams (ed.), *Letters*, 228.

218 Cropper, *Life*, 77.

219 Armstrong, *Evelyn*, 215.

220 Lillie, *Some*, 50.

221 Lillie, *Some*, 51.

222 Kelly, *Baron*, 214.

223 Von Hügel, *Reality*, 136.

224 Von Hügel, *Essays I*, 104.

225 Von Hügel, *Essays I*, 105.

226 Von Hügel, *Essays I*, 101–2.

227 G. Greene (ed.), *Niece*, xxxvi.

228 D. Greene (ed.), *Fragments*, 51.

229 Poston (ed.), *Making*, 345.

230 G. Greene (ed.), *Niece*, xvi.

231 Von Hügel, *Reality*, 145.

232 Holland (ed.), *Selected*, 137.

233 G. Greene, 'Baron', 128, 130.

234 G. Greene, 'Thoughts', 258.

235 G. Greene (ed.), *Niece*, ix–x.

236 G. Greene (ed.), *Niece*, xvii.

237 Von Hügel, *Reality*, 30.

238 Underhill, *Mixed*, 212.

239 Von Hügel, *Essays I*, 102–3.

240 G. Greene (ed.), *Niece*, 135.

241 G. Greene, 'Thoughts', 255.

242 G. Greene, 'Thoughts', 256.

243 G. Greene (ed.), *Niece*, xl, xli; G. Greene, 'Baron', 128; Underhill, 'Essence', 823; Williams (ed.), *Letters*, 129; Underhill, *Mixed*, 230, 232.

244 PA, Menzies, Unpublished MS, IX.21.

245 Holland (ed.), *Selected*, 53; G. Greene, 'Baron', 131.

246 G. Greene, 'Baron', 129; Underhill, *Mixed*, 210; Cropper, *Life*, 84.

247 Underhill, *Mixed*, 230, 233.

248 Underhill, *Mixed*, 210, 209.

249 Underhill, *Mixed*, 226; PA, Armstrong Box.

250 Underhill, *Mixed*, 210; G. Greene, *Two*, 183.

251 Underhill, *Mixed*, 230, 233.

252 Williams (ed.), *Letters*, 129; G. Greene, *Two*, 139.

253 G. Greene, 'Baron', 129.

254 Allchin, 'Foreword', in D. Greene (ed.), *Fragments*, 10; Underhill, *Mixed*, 230.

255 G. Greene (ed.), *Niece*, 27.

256 G. Greene (ed.), *Niece*, xxx.

257 G. Greene (ed.), *Niece*, 26; D. Greene (ed.), *Fragments*, 27.

258 Petre, *Tyrrell*, viii.

259 D. Greene (ed.), *Fragments*, 26.

260 Allchin, *Kingdom*, 185–6.

261 Armstrong, *Evelyn*, 229.

262 Armstrong, *Evelyn*, 213.

263 KCLA, K/PP75, 9/7, Obituary of Evelyn Underhill by Geoffrey Curtis, in *The Community of the Resurrection Chronicle*, no. 155 (1941).

264 Steere, *Counsels*, 21.

265 Michael Ramsay, 'Foreword', in Armstrong, *Evelyn*, ix.

266 Cropper, *Life*, 137; Steere, *Gleanings*, 55–6.

267 KCLA, K/PP75, 5/5, F. R. Barry's review of *The Golden Sequence*.

268 Williams (ed.), *Letters*, 255.

269 KCLA, K/PP75, 1/30/1, Letter from Olive Wyon to John Manola, 8 August 1963.

Chapter 4

1 Williams (ed.), *Letters*, 26.

2 Cropper, *Life*, 169.

3 Poston (ed.), *Making*, 85.

4 Williams (ed.), *Letters*, 51, 203.

5 Cropper, *Life*, 140; Underhill, *Ways*, 96.

6 Underhill, *Ways*, 97.

7 Poston (ed.), *Making*, 148; PA, Armstrong Box, Letter from E. I. Watkin to Daniel, 17 July 1976.

8 SAUL, MS 5552, n.d.

9 Cropper, *Life*, 107.

10 Poston (ed.), *Making*, 156.

11 Williams (ed.), *Letters*, 66; Menzies, 'Memoir', 21, 16.

12 Cropper, *Life*, 171; Williams (ed.), *Letters*, 315.

13 Williams (ed.), *Letters*, 227.

14 Cropper, *Life*, 138.

15 KCLA, K/PP75, 1/3/1.

16 KCLA, K/PP75, 1/27/15; Poston (ed.), *Making*, 271.

17 Williams (ed.), *Letters*, 232; Cropper, *Life*, 111.

18 Williams (ed.), *Letters*, 61.

19 Poston (ed.), *Making*, 113.

20 Poston (ed.), *Making*, 123, 127, 159, 133.

21 Williams (ed.), *Letters*, 174, 177.

22 Williams (ed.), *Letters*, 160; Cropper, *Life*, 139, 129.

23 Cropper, *Life*, 163.

24 Cropper, *Life*, 162.

25 Williams (ed.), *Letters*, 127.

26 D. Greene (ed.), *Fragments*, 57.

27 Williams (ed.), *Letters*, 177.

28 Steere, *Gleanings*, 69.

29 Williams (ed.), *Letters*, 45; Cropper, *Life*, 231.

30 PA, Menzies, Unpublished MS, IV.6; IX.6.

31 Williams (ed.), *Letters*, 44.

32 Armstrong, *Evelyn*, 244, 243.

33 Williams (ed.), *Letters*, 21.

34 Cropper, *Life*, 136.

35 Armstrong, *Evelyn*, 285–6.

36 Williams (ed.), *Letters*, 31; KCLA, K/PP75, 1/3/2.

37 PA, Menzies, Unpublished MS, XI.

38 Barkway, 'Evelyn', 368; Armstrong, *Evelyn*, 243.

39 PA, Menzies, Unpublished MS, IX.

40 Menzies, 'Memoir', 16; Cropper, *Life*, 245, 169.

41 KCLA, K/PP75, 9/26; Armstrong, *Evelyn*, 285; PA, Menzies, Unpublished MS, IX.

42 Cropper, *Life*, 169.

43 Cropper, *Life*, 170, 230.

44 PA, Menzies, Unpublished MS, VI.9, 15.

45 Williams (ed.), *Letters*, 140, 130.

46 Williams (ed.), *Letters*, 147, 163; Cropper, *Life*, 203.

47 Williams (ed.), *Letters*, 239–40.

48 Poston (ed.), *Making*, 235, 232, 241.

49 Williams (ed.), *Letters*, 226, 270, 271.

50 Poston (ed.), *Making*, 232, 229.

51 Williams (ed.), *Letters*, 220.

52 Poston (ed.), *Making*, 303.

53 Poston (ed.), *Making*, 316, 231, 289.

54 KCLA, K/PP75, 5/9, Review of Williams (ed.), *Letters*, by Theodora Bosanquet, in *Time and Tide* (15 January 1944); Review of Williams (ed.), *Letters*, by F. J. Rae, in *The Expository Times* (February 1944).

55 KCLA, K/PP75, 5/10, 'The On Shining of Glory', *The Guardian*.

56 Williams (ed.), *Letters*, 256.

57 Williams (ed.), *Letters*, 230.

58 Poston (ed.), *Making*, 230.

59 Poston (ed.), *Making*, 146.

60 Poston (ed.), *Making*, 148.

61 Williams (ed.), *Letters*, 270.

62 Williams (ed.), *Letters*, 57, 212.

63 Poston (ed.), *Making*, 100.

64 Williams (ed.), *Letters*, 92, 91.

65 Menzies, 'Memoir', 17.
66 KCLA, K/PP75, 5/9, de la Bédoyère, 'A Great Anglican'.
67 Poston (ed.), *Making*, x, xvi.
68 Cropper, *Life*, 194.
69 Williams (ed.), *Letters*, 162–3.
70 Poston (ed.), *Making*, 105, 150, 231.
71 Williams (ed.), *Letters*, 338; Cropper, *Life*, 204; Poston (ed.), *Making*, 193, 245.
72 Williams (ed.), *Letters*, 86.
73 Williams (ed.), *Letters*, 213, 245.
74 Poston (ed.), *Making*, 230.
75 Williams (ed.), *Letters*, 319.
76 Williams (ed.), *Letters*, 225, 230, 232, 237, 238, 221, 170.
77 Poston (ed.), *Making*, 229.
78 Williams (ed.), *Letters*, 156, 152–3; Poston (ed.), *Making*, 234; Williams (ed.), *Letters*, 183, 242, 184.
79 Poston (ed.), *Making*, 229, 239.
80 Williams (ed.), *Letters*, 64, 240; Poston (ed.), *Making*, 103, 233, 261, 232.
81 Williams (ed.), *Letters*, 104, 168, 191; Poston (ed.), *Making*, 233.
82 KCLA, K/PP75, 1/18/3, 22 July 1945.
83 Menzies (ed.), *Collected*, 154; Underhill, *Concerning*, 52.
84 Menzies (ed.), *Collected*, 154.
85 Menzies (ed.), *Collected*, 122.
86 Menzies (ed.), *Collected*, 123.
87 Menzies (ed.), *Collected*, 123, 156.
88 Underhill, *Concerning*, 52.
89 Holland (ed.), *Selected*, 147.
90 Huvelin, *Guides*, 11; Menzies (ed.), *Collected*, 154.
91 Menzies (ed.), *Collected*, 154–5; Cropper, *Life*, 169; Underhill, *Concerning*, 53.
92 Underhill, *Concerning*, 54–5.
93 Underhill, *Concerning*, 59.
94 Underhill, *Direction*, 7.
95 Menzies (ed.), *Collected*, 29–30.
96 Menzies (ed.), *Collected*, 155.
97 Williams (ed.), *Letters*, 200; Menzies (ed.), *Collected*, 156.
98 Underhill, *Concerning*, 56–7, 58.
99 Underhill, *Concerning*, 52–3.
100 Williams (ed.), *Letters*, 164, 175, 226, 232; Poston (ed.), *Making*, 229.
101 Williams (ed.), *Letters*, 242.
102 Williams (ed.), *Letters*, 143.
103 Underhill, *Fruits*, 71; Poston (ed.), *Making*, 234.
104 Williams (ed.), *Letters*, 215, 127, 184, 195.

105 Poston (ed.), *Making*, 337, 300, 243.
106 Williams (ed.), *Letters*, 245, 173.
107 Williams (ed.), *Letters*, 194, 173.
108 Poston (ed.), *Making*, 313.
109 Williams (ed.), *Letters*, 201–2, 252; Poston (ed.), *Making*, 313; Williams (ed.), *Letters*, 185.
110 Williams (ed.), *Letters*, 248, 244.
111 Poston (ed.), *Making*, 314, 253; Williams (ed.), *Letters*, 258.
112 Poston (ed.), *Making*, 241.
113 Williams (ed.), *Letters*, 51.
114 Williams (ed.), *Letters*, 213.
115 Williams (ed.), *Letters*, 84, 190, 194; Underhill, *Ways*, 112.
116 Williams (ed.), *Letters*, 120, 195, 247, 133; Poston (ed.), *Making*, 312.
117 Poston (ed.), *Making*, 312; Williams (ed.), *Letters*, 264.
118 Williams (ed.), *Letters*, 132, 231, 190, 194; Poston (ed.), *Making*, 312.
119 Underhill, 'Degrees', 8.
120 Underhill, 'Degrees', 8.
121 Poston (ed.), *Making*, 316; Williams (ed.), *Letters*, 218, 34, 248.
122 Williams (ed.), *Letters*, 271.
123 Williams (ed.), *Letters*, 270–1, 171.
124 Williams (ed.), *Letters*, 247.
125 Poston (ed.), *Making*, 316; Williams (ed.), *Letters*, 171.
126 Williams (ed.), *Letters*, 70.
127 Williams (ed.), *Letters*, 247, 241.
128 Williams (ed.), *Letters*, 194.
129 Poston (ed.), *Making*, 243; Williams (ed.), *Letters*, 234.
130 Williams (ed.), *Letters*, 340.
131 Williams (ed.), *Letters*, 179; Poston (ed.), *Making*, 327.
132 Poston (ed.), *Making*, 327; Williams (ed.), *Letters*, 175–6, 244–5.
133 Williams (ed.), *Letters*, 328.
134 Williams (ed.), *Letters*, 270–1.
135 Williams (ed.), *Letters*, 273.
136 Williams (ed.), *Letters*, 258, 165–6.
137 Williams (ed.), *Letters*, 107.
138 Williams (ed.), *Letters*, 326, 92.
139 Williams (ed.), *Letters*, 209.
140 Williams (ed.), *Letters*, 212, 224.
141 Poston (ed.), *Making*, 235.

142 Williams (ed.), *Letters*, 73, 271.

143 Williams (ed.), *Letters*, 127.

144 Cropper, *Life*, 231.

145 Williams (ed.), *Letters*, 79, 120, 105.

146 Williams (ed.), *Letters*, 123, 89.

147 Poston (ed.), *Making*, 162, 254.

148 Williams (ed.), *Letters*, 260, 224–5, 172.

149 Williams (ed.), *Letters*, 239.

150 Williams (ed.), *Letters*, 172, 90; Poston (ed.), *Making*, 302.

151 Williams (ed.), *Letters*, 231.

152 Williams (ed.), *Letters*, 177; Poston (ed.), *Making*, 262, 302.

153 Williams (ed.), *Letters*, 253; Poston (ed.), *Making*, 243.

154 Poston (ed.), *Making*, 311, 256; Williams (ed.), *Letters*, 172.

155 Williams (ed.), *Letters*, 172, 120.

156 Williams (ed.), *Letters*, 170.

157 Williams (ed.), *Letters*, 230, 223; Poston (ed.), *Making*, 231.

158 Williams (ed.), *Letters*, 172.

159 Williams (ed.), *Letters*, 121.

160 Williams (ed.), *Letters*, 174.

161 Poston (ed.), *Making*, 311.

162 Williams (ed.), *Letters*, 219.

163 Williams (ed.), *Letters*, 207, 224, 231, 239.

164 Williams (ed.), *Letters*, 221, 225.

165 Poston (ed.), *Making*, 262.

166 Poston (ed.), *Making*, 300.

167 Williams (ed.), *Letters*, 240.

168 Williams (ed.), *Letters*, 191, 168.

169 Williams (ed.), *Letters*, 63, 155.

170 Poston (ed.), *Making*, 230.

171 Williams (ed.), *Letters*, 168, 195, 260.

172 Williams (ed.), *Letters*, 182, 172, 178.

173 Williams (ed.), *Letters*, 103, 231, 319, 333, 169, 168.

174 Williams (ed.), *Letters*, 168.

175 Williams (ed.), *Letters*, 237.

176 Steere, *Dimensions*, 115.

177 Williams (ed.), *Letters*, 165–6, 260.

178 Williams (ed.), *Letters*, 96–7.

179 Williams (ed.), *Letters*, 274–5.

180 Williams (ed.), *Letters*, 152.

181 Williams (ed.), *Letters*, 132; PA, Menzies, Unpublished MS, XI.8.

182 Williams (ed.), *Letters*, 189, 272–3.

183 Poston (ed.), *Making*, 351.

184 Williams (ed.), *Letters*, 211, 192.

185 Williams (ed.), *Letters*, 222, 264.

186 Williams (ed.), *Letters*, 207–8, 84.

187 Poston (ed.), *Making*, 258.

188 Williams (ed.), *Letters*, 96.

189 Poston (ed.), *Making*, 255.

190 Williams (ed.), *Letters*, 243; Poston (ed.), *Making*, 156, 251.

191 Williams (ed.), *Letters*, 72, 232, 96, 66, 88; Poston (ed.), *Making*, 139, 245.

192 Poston (ed.), *Making*, 104, 251.

193 Williams (ed.), *Letters*, 66.

194 Williams (ed.), *Letters*, 237.

195 Williams (ed.), *Letters*, 131–2.

196 Williams (ed.), *Letters*, 259.

197 Williams (ed.), *Letters*, 218, 228, 258.

198 Poston (ed.), *Making*, 251.

199 Williams (ed.), *Letters*, 227, 88.

200 Poston (ed.), *Making*, 250, 123, 316; Williams (ed.), *Letters*, 64, 68, 87, 169, 240, 122, 64.

201 Williams (ed.), *Letters*, 163, 220, 245, 240; Poston (ed.), *Making*, 248.

202 Williams (ed.), *Letters*, 163.

203 Williams (ed.), *Letters*, 213, 218.

204 Williams (ed.), *Letters*, 243, 200; Poston (ed.), *Making*, 247.

205 Williams (ed.), *Letters*, 240, 184, 64, 127, 190, 242, 156, 184, 242.

206 Poston (ed.), *Making*, 332, 333, 345, 270, 307, 327.

207 Williams (ed.), *Letters*, 184.

208 Williams (ed.), *Letters*, 271, 242.

209 Cropper, *Life*, 197; Poston (ed.), *Making*, 231–2, 261.

210 Williams (ed.), *Letters*, 216, 168–9; Poston (ed.), *Making*, 232.

211 Williams (ed.), *Letters*, 182, 184, 272–3, 155, 191; Poston (ed.), *Making*, 253.

212 Williams (ed.), *Letters*, 86.

213 Williams (ed.), *Letters*, 122.

214 KCLA, K/PP75, 9/5, Obituary of Evelyn Underhill by Lucy Menzies, in *Chelmsford Diocesan Chronicle* (1941), 93–4.

215 PA, Menzies, Unpublished MS, VI.11; Cropper, *Life*, 169.

216 Williams (ed.), *Letters*, 38.

217 Poston (ed.), *Making*, 236, 234.

218 Poston (ed.), *Making*, 325.

219 Williams (ed.), *Letters*, 92–3.

220 Williams (ed.), *Letters*, 149, 173, 90, 227, 219.

221 Williams (ed.), *Letters*, 173–4, 176.

222 Williams (ed.), *Letters*, 149.

223 Cropper, *Life*, 174; Williams (ed.), *Letters*, 220, 218.

224 Williams (ed.), *Letters*, 168; Poston (ed.), *Making*, 273.

225 Armstrong, *Evelyn*, 285; Williams (ed.), *Letters*, 169, 187.

226 Poston (ed.), *Making*, 245, 345; Williams (ed.), *Letters*, 79–80.

227 Poston (ed.), *Making*, 243, 248; Williams (ed.), *Letters*, 64.

228 Williams (ed.), *Letters*, 222, 72, 229.

229 Williams (ed.), *Letters*, 104, 121.

230 Poston (ed.), *Making*, 345.

231 Williams (ed.), *Letters*, 240.

232 Williams (ed.), *Letters*, 72.

233 Williams (ed.), *Letters*, 249.

234 Williams (ed.), *Letters*, 178, 250.

235 Poston (ed.), *Making*, 230; Williams (ed.), *Letters*, 316.

236 Williams (ed.), *Letters*, 226, 123.

237 Williams (ed.), *Letters*, 92, 227, 232.

238 Williams (ed.), *Letters*, 220, 304–5.

239 Williams (ed.), *Letters*, 228; Poston (ed.), *Making*, 326.

240 Poston (ed.), *Making*, 311.

241 Williams (ed.), *Letters*, 153, 118.

242 Williams (ed.), *Letters*, 314.

243 Williams (ed.), *Letters*, 314–15.

244 Poston (ed.), *Making*, 327.

245 Williams (ed.), *Letters*, 337.

246 Williams (ed.), *Letters*, 192, 187.

247 Poston (ed.), *Making*, 304; Williams (ed.), *Letters*, 175; PA, Menzies, Unpublished MS, IX.

248 Williams (ed.), *Letters*, 79.

249 Williams (ed.), *Letters*, 216, 217–18, 97, 222, 219.

250 Williams (ed.), *Letters*, 83–4; Poston (ed.), *Making*, 113.

251 Williams (ed.), *Letters*, 124, 256, 250.

252 Williams (ed.), *Letters*, 250.

253 Williams (ed.), *Letters*, 97.

254 Williams (ed.), *Letters*, 81, 165–6.

255 Williams (ed.), *Letters*, 206, 69, 262, 188.

256 Williams (ed.), *Letters*, 120, 200.
257 Williams (ed.), *Letters*, 131, 147, 67.
258 Williams (ed.), *Letters*, 92.
259 Williams (ed.), *Letters*, 188.
260 Williams (ed.), *Letters*, 82.
261 Williams (ed.), *Letters*, 204.
262 Williams (ed.), *Letters*, 253.
263 Williams (ed.), *Letters*, 190.
264 Williams (ed.), *Letters*, 191.
265 Poston (ed.), *Making*, 240; Williams (ed.), *Letters*, 97.
266 Williams (ed.), *Letters*, 231.
267 Poston (ed.), *Making*, 128.
268 Williams (ed.), *Letters*, 253.
269 Williams (ed.), *Letters*, 252, 82.
270 Williams (ed.), *Letters*, 241–2.
271 Williams (ed.), *Letters*, 253.
272 Williams (ed.), *Letters*, 81; Poston (ed.), *Making*, 298.
273 KCLA, K/PP75, 1/15/148, 149.
274 KCLA, K/PP75, 1/18/8; PA, Menzies, Unpublished MS, XI.
275 KCLA, K/PP75, 1/3/2.
276 Cropper, *Life*, 246.
277 Gardner, *Composition*, 69–70.
278 Poston (ed.), *Making*, 160.

Chapter 5

1 Williams (ed.), *Letters*, 339.
2 Poston (ed.), *Making*, x.
3 Cropper, *Life*, 124.
4 D. Greene (ed.), *Fragments*, 113.
5 D. Greene (ed.), *Fragments*, 46.
6 Cropper, *Life*, 122.
7 Menzies, 'Memoir', 11; Underhill, *Fruits*, 12; Cropper, *Life*, 121, 184.
8 Williams (ed.), *Letters*, 210.
9 Williams (ed.), *Letters*, 30.
10 Armstrong, *Evelyn*, 266.
11 Cropper, *Life*, 167.
12 Williams (ed.), *Letters*, 237.
13 Steere, *Gleanings*, 69.
14 Underhill, *Ways*, 38; Williams (ed.), *Letters*, 30.
15 Cropper, *Life*, 194.
16 Cropper, *Life*, 200.
17 Cropper, *Life*, 218; Armstrong, *Evelyn*, 286.
18 Cropper, *Life*, 214, 223.
19 Underhill, *Spiritual*, 63; Cropper, *Life*, 223.
20 KCLA, K/PP75, 9/6.
21 Menzies, 'Memoir', 22.
22 D. Greene (ed.), *Fragments*, 59.
23 D. Greene (ed.), *Fragments*, 59.
24 Cropper, *Life*, 131.
25 Williams (ed.), *Letters*, 173; Cropper, *Life*, 187.
26 Williams (ed.), *Letters*, 205.
27 Allchin, *Friendship*, 35.

28 Cropper, *Life*, 131; Williams (ed.), *Letters*, 163.

29 Cropper, *Life*, 131.

30 Cropper, *Life*, 181.

31 Cropper, *Life*, 193, 199; Williams (ed.), *Letters*, 340.

32 Cropper, *Life*, 164.

33 Steere, *Gleanings*, 68.

34 Cropper, *Life*, 167.

35 Cropper, *Life*, 167–8.

36 Poston (ed.), *Making*, 268.

37 Underhill, *Light*, 106.

38 Underhill, *Ways*, 164.

39 Cropper, *Life*, 167–8.

40 Menzies, 'Memoir', 12.

41 Cropper, *Life*, 168.

42 KCLA, K/PP75, 9/10, 'The Writings of Evelyn Underhill: A critical analysis', by Sr Mary Xavier Kirby, 1965.

43 Underhill, *Ways*, 36.

44 Underhill, *Ways*, 37.

45 Underhill, *Ways*, 108.

46 Underhill, *Ways*, 154.

47 Underhill, *Ways*, 52; Armstrong, *Evelyn*, 272.

48 Cropper, *Life*, 168, 150.

49 Cropper, *Life*, 193.

50 Underhill, *Meditations*, 3.

51 Underhill, *Meditations*, 3–4.

52 Underhill, *Ways*, 108.

53 Wrigley-Carr (ed.), *Evelyn*.

54 Williams (ed.), *Letters*, 333.

55 Underhill, *Ways*, 39.

56 Cropper, *Life*, 168.

57 Loades, *Evelyn*, 11.

58 Underhill, *Light*, 88; Underhill, *Ways*, 159.

59 Underhill, *Ways*, 166; Leonard, *Creative*, 110.

60 Underhill, *Ways*, 36.

61 Cropper, *Life*, 179–80.

62 Cropper, *Life*, 147.

63 Poston (ed.), *Making*, 264; Armstrong, *Evelyn*, 275.

64 PA, Darcie Otter Box.

65 Poston (ed.), *Making*, 248–9.

66 Williams (ed.), *Letters*, 163.

67 Menzies, 'Memoir', 10.

68 KCLA, K/PP75, 1/3/2, 13 August 1962; Cropper, *Life*, 168.

69 Cropper, *Life*, 168; Steere, *Gleanings*, 68.

70 Underhill, *Fruits*, 2.

71 Underhill, *Fruits*, 2; Underhill, *Ways*, 238.

72 Von Hügel, *Essays II*, 246–7.

73 Underhill, *Light*, 25.

74 Underhill, *Spiritual*, 36–7.

75 Underhill, *Light*, 105–6; Underhill, *Ways*, 238.

76 Steere, *Gleanings*, 68.

77 Menzies, 'Memoir', 16; Underhill, *Ways*, 109; Underhill, *Fruits*, 1.

78 Underhill, *Light*, 102.

79 Underhill, *Light*, 102–3.

80 Underhill, *Light*, 103.

81 Underhill, *Ways*, 106–7; Underhill, *Light*, 104–5.

82 Underhill, *Light*, 106–7.

83 Underhill, *Ways*, 55.

84 Underhill, *Ways*, 55.

85 Underhill, *Ways*, 107.

86 Underhill, *Ways*, 161.

87 Underhill, *Ways*, 72, 99.

88 Underhill, *Ways*, 152.

89 Poston (ed.), *Making*, 241; Underhill, *Ways*, 50–1.

90 Underhill, *Ways*, 50–1; Underhill, *Light*, 25–6.

91 Underhill, *Ways*, 50.

92 Underhill, *Ways*, 50–1.

93 Underhill, *Ways*, 106.

94 Underhill, *Ways*, 51.

95 Underhill, *Fruits*, 3; Underhill, *Light*, 28.

96 Underhill, *Ways*, 149.

97 Underhill, *Ways*, 57.

98 Underhill, *Ways*, 176.

99 Underhill, *Ways*, 93, 121.

100 Underhill, *Ways*, 90, 72.

101 Underhill, Ways, 90–1.

102 Underhill, *Light*, 65–6, 26–7; Underhill, *Ways*, 55.

103 Underhill, *Concerning*, 26; Underhill, *Light*, 27.

104 Underhill, *Light*, 33–4; Underhill, *Ways*, 91.

105 Underhill, *Ways*, 53, 118.

106 Underhill, *Concerning*, 28; Underhill, *Ways*, 199.

107 Underhill, *Ways*, 176, 56; Underhill, *Fruits*, 3.

108 Underhill, *Ways*, 119, 120–1.

109 Underhill, *Mount*, 258.

110 Underhill, *Concerning*, 25.

111 Underhill, *Supernatural*, 204; Underhill, *Ways*, 111.

112 Menzies, 'Memoir', 15.

113 Underhill, *Ways*, 175, 142.

114 Underhill, *Ways*, 136; Underhill, *Concerning*, 7.

115 Underhill, *Ways*, 113.

116 Underhill, *Concerning*, 9; Underhill, *Ways*, 136.

117 Underhill, *Ways*, 136; Underhill, *Concerning*, 26.

118 Underhill, *Ways*, 136, 177.

119 Underhill, *Concerning*, 27, 29.

120 Underhill, *Concerning*, 4.

121 Underhill, *Ways*, 181.

122 Underhill, *Concerning*, 13, 8, 38.

123 Underhill, *Concerning*, 4, 13, 12; Underhill, *Light*, 54.

124 Underhill, *Ways*, 187.

125 Underhill, *Ways*, 137, 191; Underhill, *Light*, 25, 33.

126 Underhill, *Ways*, 136.

127 Underhill, *Light*, 33;
Underhill, *Ways*, 189.

128 Underhill, *Ways*, 190–1.

129 Underhill, *Light*, 61–2;
Underhill, *Ways*, 78.

130 Underhill, *Concerning*, 44,
51.

131 Underhill, *Light*, 77;
Underhill, *Ways*, 79.

132 Underhill, *Ways*, 77, 138.

133 Underhill, *Ways*, 135;
Underhill, *Concerning*, 23.

134 Underhill, *Ways*, 77, 80.

135 Underhill, *Concerning*, 39.

136 Underhill, *Concerning*, 40.

137 Underhill, *Concerning*, 37.

138 Underhill, *Concerning*, 38, 44.

139 Underhill, *Ways*, 172.

140 Underhill, *Concerning*, 38.

141 Underhill, *Ways*, 85;
Underhill, *Concerning*, 31.

142 Underhill, *Ways*, 178.

143 Underhill, *Light*, 39, 56;
Underhill, *Ways*, 114.

144 Underhill, *Ways*, 112, 179.

145 Underhill, *Concerning*, 24, 30.

146 Underhill, *Ways*, 137, 135,
138.

147 Underhill, *Concerning*, 36, 21.

148 Underhill, *Light*, 43–4.

149 Underhill, *Light*, 44, 45–6.

150 Underhill, *Ways*, 73, 91;
Underhill, *Light*, 33.

151 Underhill, *Ways*, 92;
Underhill, *Light*, 50, 51.

152 Underhill, *Ways*, 93–4;
Underhill, *Light*, 32.

153 Underhill, *Light*, 32.

154 Underhill, *Light*, 46.

155 Underhill, *Light*, 46, 55.

156 Underhill, *Light*, 50;
Underhill, *Ways*, 96–7.

157 Underhill, *Light*, 37, 47–8.

158 Underhill, *Ways*, 138;
Underhill, *Light*, 50, 63.

159 Underhill, *Light*, 49, 64.

160 Underhill, *Ways*, 61.

161 Underhill, *Ways*, 98;
Underhill, *Light*, 84, 83.

162 Underhill, *Ways*, 170, 169.

163 Underhill, *Ways*, 65, 73.

164 Underhill, *Ways*, 83–4.

165 Underhill, *Ways*, 84.

166 Underhill, *Ways*, 85–6.

167 Cropper, *Life*, 150; Underhill,
Ways, 182.

168 Underhill, *Ways*, 62, 117, 222.

169 Williams (ed.), *Letters*, 219;
Poston (ed.), *Making*, 233.

170 Underhill, *Ways*, 150, 167;
Poston (ed.), *Making*, 334.

171 Cropper, *Life*, 150.

172 KCLA, K/PP75, 3/4/16, 'The
Way of Renewal'.

173 KCLA, K/PP75, 9/5, Obituary
of Evelyn Underhill by Lucy

Menzies, in *Chelmsford Diocesan Chronicle* (1941), 93–4.

174 Cropper, *Life*, 246.

175 Cropper, *Life*, 167.

176 Williams (ed.), *Letters*, 200.

177 Wrigley-Carr (ed.), *Evelyn*, 14.

Afterword

1 Peterson, *Resurrection*, 182, 252; Peterson, *Pastor*, 224.

2 Email from Eugene Peterson to the author, 22 September 2015; Peterson, *Resurrection*, 184.

3 Letters from Eugene Peterson to the author, 4 February 2007, 15 December 2012; Peterson, *Resurrection*, 183.

4 Peterson, *Resurrection*, 277.

5 Letters from Eugene Peterson to the author, 12 May 2007, 4 July 2008.

6 Peterson, *Pastor*, 224; Letters from Eugene Peterson to the author, 12 May 2007, 3 March 2008.

7 Letter from Eugene Peterson to the author, 12 May 2007.

8 Letter from Eugene Peterson to the author, 12 May 2007.

9 Peterson, *Pastor*, 225–6.

10 Peterson, *Pastor*, 226.

11 Peterson, *Resurrection*, 273–4.

12 Peterson, *Resurrection*, 5.

13 Underhill, *Mixed*, 230.

14 Letter from Eugene Peterson to the author, 3 March 2008.

15 G. Greene, *Two*, 101.

References

Where two or more references are provided in a single endnote, the sources relate to material directly quoted or paraphrased in the preceding sentence(s) in the order in which it appears. Emphases in quotations are original unless otherwise stated.

DAA Downside Abbey Archive
KCLA King's College London Archives, Evelyn Underhill
PA Pleshey Archive
SAUL St Andrews University Library, Special Collections

Friendship Allchin, A. M., *Friendship in God*. Oxford: SLG Press, 2003.

Kingdom Allchin, A. M., *The Kingdom of Love and Knowledge*. New York: Seabury Press, 1982.

Evelyn Armstrong, Christopher, *Evelyn Underhill (1875–1941): An introduction to her life and writings*. London: Mowbrays, 1975.

Writings Augustine of Hippo, *Selected Writings*, ed. Emilie Griffin, trans. Mary T. Clark. New York: Paulist Press, 1984.

'Evelyn' Barkway, Lumsden, Bishop, 'Great Pastors – X. Evelyn Underhill', *Theology* (October 1953): 368–72.

'**Baron**' Barmann, Lawrence, 'Baron Friedrich von Hügel as a Religious Genius.' *The Ampleforth Journal* 77: Part 3 (1972): 64–8.

Letters Barmann, Lawrence (ed.), *The Letters of Baron Friedrich von Hügel and Professor Norman Kemp Smith*. New York: Fordham University Press, 1981.

'**Modernist**' Barmann, Lawrence, 'The modernist as mystic.' In Darryl Rodock (ed.), *Catholicism Contending with Modernity: Roman Catholic modernism and anti-modernism in historical context*, 213–47. Cambridge: Cambridge University Press, 2000.

Frances Barrows, Mary Prentice Lillie, *Frances Crane Lillie (1969– 1958): A memoir*. Chicago, IL: Smith College Library, 1969.

'**Sense**' Beattie, J.W., 'The sense of the infinite in the philosophy of religion of Friedrich von Hügel'. PhD, Université Catholique de Louvain, 1969.

'**Friedrich**' Butler, Dom Cuthbert, 'Friedrich von Hügel'. In *Religions of Authority and the Religion of the Spirit*, 179–85. London: Sheed & Ward, 1930.

New Campbell, R. J., *The New Theology*. London: Clarendon Press, 1929.

Spiritual Chapman, Dom, *Spiritual Letters*. London: Burns & Oates, 1934,

Life Cropper, Margaret, *The Life of Evelyn Underhill*. Woodstock, VT: SkyLight Paths, 2003.

Laughter D'Arcy, M. S., SJ, *Laughter and the Love of Friends*. Westminster, MD: Christian Classics, 1991.

Life De la Bédoyère, Michael, *The Life of Baron von Hügel*. New York: Charles Scribner's Sons, 1951.

Little Garceau, Eduoard, *The Little Doustes*, trans. Vera A. Chappell. London: Frederick Muller, 1935.

Composition Gardner, Helen, *The Composition of Four Quartets*. London: Faber & Faber, 1978.

'**Friedrich**' Gibbard, Mark, 'Friedrich von Hügel – scholar'. In *Twentieth-Century Men of Prayer*, 12–23. London: SCM Press, 1975.

'**Ward**' Goodacre, N. W., 'Ward, Reginald Somerset.' In Gordon S. Wakefield (ed.), *The Westminster Dictionary of Christian Spirituality*, 389. Louisville, KY: Westminster John Knox Press, 1983.

Artist Greene, Dana, *Evelyn Underhill: Artist of the infinite life*. London: Darton, Longman & Todd, 1991.

Fragments Greene, Dana (ed.), *Fragments from an Inner Life: The notebooks of Evelyn Underhill*. Harrisburg, PA: Morehouse, 1993.

Guide Greene, Dana (ed.), *Evelyn Underhill: Modern guide to the ancient quest for the holy*. New York: State University of New York Press, 1988.

'Baron' Greene, Gwendolen, 'Baron Friedrich von Hügel'. *Pax*, 24 (154) (September 1932): 128–32.

Niece Greene, Gwendolen (ed.), *Letters from Baron Friedrich von Hügel to a Niece*. London: J. M. Dent & Sons, 1927.

'Recollections' Greene, Gwendolen, 'Some recollections of Baron von Hügel'. *The Spectator*, 143 (1929): 148–9.

'Thoughts' Greene, Gwendolen, 'Thoughts from Baron von Hügel'. *Dublin Review* (April–June 1931): 254–60.

Two Greene, Gwendolen, *Two Witnesses*. London: J. M. Dent & Sons, 1930.

'Memoir' Holland, Bernard, 'Memoir'. In Bernard Holland (ed.), *Baron Friedrich von Hügel: Selected Letters, 1896–1924*, 1–57. London: J. M. Dent & Sons, 1927.

Selected Holland, Bernard (ed.), *Baron Friedrich von Hügel: Selected letters, 1896–1924*. London: J. M. Dent & Sons, 1926.

Addresses Huvelin, Henri, *Addresses to Women*. London: Burns, Oates & Washbourne, 1936.

Guides Huvelin, Henri, *Some Spiritual Guides of the Seventeenth Century*. London: Burns & Oates, 1927.

Baron Kelly, James J., *Baron Friedrich von Hügel's Philosophy of Religion*. Leuven: Leuven University Press, 1983.

'Friend' Kelly, James J., 'Von Hügel to a friend.' *The Tablet*, 229 (January 1975): 78–9.

Letters Kelly, James J. (ed.), *The Letters of Baron Friedrich von Hügel and Maude D. Petre: The modernist movement in England*. Leuven: Peeters, 2003.

Creative Leonard, Ellen M., *Creative Tension*. Chicago, IL: University of Chicago Press, 1997.

Religious Lester-Garland, L. V., *The Religious Philosophy of Baron Friedrich von Hügel*. London: J. M. Dent & Sons, 1934.

Some Lillie, Frances, *Some Letters of Baron von Hügel*. Privately printed, 1925.

Evelyn Loades, Ann, *Evelyn Underhill*. London: Fount, 1997.

Abbé Louis-Lefebvre, Marie-Thérèse, *Abbé Huvelin, Apostle of Paris, 1939–1910*. Paris: Clonmore & Reynolds, 1967.

'Letter' Mansel, Juliet, 'A Letter from Baron Friedrich von Hügel'. *The Dublin Review* 222 (452) (July 1951): 1–11.

Collected Menzies, Lucy (ed.), *Collected Papers of Evelyn Underhill*. London: Longmans, Green & Co, 1946.

'Memoir' Menzies, Lucy, 'Memoir', in Evelyn Underhill, *The Fruits of the Spirit*, 9–22. London: Longmans, 1960.

Friedrich Misner, Paul, *Friedrich von Hügel, Nathan Söderblom, Friedrich Heiler: Briefwechsel, 1909–1931*. Konfessionskundliche Schriften des Johann-Adam-Möhler Instituts 14. Paderborn: VerlagBonifatius-Druckerei, 1981.

Reginald Morgan, Edmund R., *Reginald Somerset Ward, 1881–1962*. London: Mowbray, 1963.

Baron Nédoncelle, Maurice. *Baron Friedrich von Hügel: A study of his life and thought*. New York: Longmans, 1937.

Pastor Peterson, Eugene, *The Pastor*. Colorado Springs, CO: HarperOne, 2011.

Resurrection Peterson, Eugene, *Practice Resurrection*. Downers Grove, IL: Eerdmans, 2010.

Tyrrell Petre, Maude, *Von Hügel and Tyrrell: The story of a friendship*. London: J. M. Dent & Sons, 1937.

Way Petre, Maude, *My Way of Faith*. London: J. M. Dent & Sons, 1937.

Making Poston, Carol (ed.), *The Making of a Mystic: New and selected letters of Evelyn Underhill*. Champaign: University of Illinois Press, 2010.

Counsels Steere, Douglas. *Spiritual Counsels and Letters of Baron Friedrich von Hügel*. London: Darton, Longman & Todd, 1964.

Dimensions Steere, Douglas, *Dimensions of Prayer*. New York: Harper & Row, 1962.

Doors Steere, Douglas, *Doors into Life*. New York: Harper & Bros, 1948.

Gleanings Steere, Douglas V., *Gleanings*. Nashville, TN: The Upper Room, 1986.

Together Steere, Douglas, *Together in Solitude*. New York: Crossroad, 1985.

Diversity Steuart, R. H., SJ, 'The Abbé Huvelin'. In *Diversity in Holiness*, 150–6. London: Sheed & Ward, 1938.

Change Underhill, Arthur, *Change and Decay: The recollections and reflections of an octogenarian bencher*. London: Butterworth & Co., 1938.

'Cant' Underhill, Evelyn, 'The cant of unconventionality. A rejoinder to Lady Robert Cecil'. *National Review*, 229 (January 1908): 755.

Church Underhill, Evelyn, *The Mystics of the Church*. London: James Clarke & Co., 1925.

Concerning Underhill, Evelyn. *Concerning the Inner Life*. London: Methuen, 1950.

'Degrees' Underhill, Evelyn, 'The degrees of prayer'. In Lucy Menzies (ed.), *Collected Papers of Evelyn Underhill*, 35–53. London: Longmans, Green, 1949.

Direction Underhill, Evelyn, 'Introduction'. In Henri de Tourville, *Letters of Direction: Thoughts on the spiritual life from the letters of the Abbé de Tourville*, 7–10. London: Dacre Press, 1961.

Eastern Underhill, Evelyn, 'Introduction'. In Nicholas Arseniew, *Mysticism and the Eastern Church*, London: Student Christian Movement, 1926.

'Essence' Underhill, Evelyn, 'The essence of von Hügel'. *The Spectator*, 141 (December 1928): 822–3.

Fruits Underhill, Evelyn, *The Fruits of the Spirit*. London: Longmans, 1960.

'Future' Underhill, Evelyn, 'The future of mysticism'. *Everyman*, 12 (301) (20 July 1918): 335–6.

Grey Underhill, Evelyn, *The Grey World*. London: William Heinemann, 1904.

Immanence Underhill, Evelyn, *Immanence*. London: J. M. Dent & Sons, 1913.

Light Underhill, Evelyn, *Light of Christ*. London: Longmans, Green, 1944.

'**Magic**' Underhill, Evelyn, 'A defence of magic'. *Fortnightly Review*, 88 (November 1907): 764–5.

Meditations Underhill, Evelyn, *Meditations and Prayers*. London: Longmans, Green & Co., 1949.

Mixed Underhill, Evelyn, *Mixed Pastures*. New York: Books for Libraries, 1933.

'**Modern**' Underhill, Evelyn, Review of *Mysticism and Modern Life* by J. W. Buckham, and of *Mysticism and the Creed* by W. F. Cobbs. *The Harvard Theological Review*, 9 (2) (April 1916): 234–8.

Mount Underhill, Evelyn, *The Mount of Purification*. London: Longmans, 1960.

Mysticism Underhill, Evelyn, *Mysticism*. New York: Doubleday, 1990.

Peace Underhill, Evelyn, *A Meditation on Peace*. London: Fellowship of Reconciliation, 1939.

Shrines Underhill, Evelyn, *Shrines and Cities of France and Italy*. London: Longmans, Green and Co., 1949.

Spirit Underhill, Evelyn, *The Life of the Spirit and the Life of Today*. Harrisburg, PA: Morehouse, 1994.

Spiritual Underhill, Evelyn, *The Spiritual Life*. Manly, NSW: Centre for Christian Spirituality, 1976.

Supernatural Underhill, Evelyn, *Man and the Supernatural*. London: Methuen, 1934.

'**War**' Underhill, Evelyn, 'The Church and war'. In Dana Greene (ed.). *Evelyn Underhill: Modern guide to the ancient quest for the holy*, 211–18. New York: State University of New York Press, 1988.

Ways Underhill, Evelyn, *The Ways of the Spirit*, ed. Grace Adolphsen Brame. New York: Crossroad, 1994.

Worship Underhill, Evelyn, *Worship*. London: Nisbet & Co., 1941.

'Apologist' von Hügel, Friedrich, 'Apologist of Religion'. *The Times Literary Supplement*, 1040 (22 December 1921): 860.

Essays I von Hügel, Friedrich, *Essays and Addresses on the Philosophy of Religion, First Series*. London: J. M. Dent & Sons, 1921.

Essays II von Hügel, Friedrich, *Essays and Addresses on the Philosophy of Religion, Second Series*, ed. Edmund Gardner. London: J. M. Dent & Sons, 1926.

Eternal von Hügel, Friedrich, *Eternal Life: A study of its implications and applications*. Edinburgh: T. & T. Clark, 1912.

German von Hügel, Friedrich, *The German Soul*. London: J. M. Dent & Sons, 1916.

'Louis' von Hügel, Friedrich, 'Louis Duchesne'. *The Times Literary Supplement* (25 May 1922): 342.

Mystical von Hügel, Friedrich, *The Mystical Element of Religion*, vols 1 and 2. London: J. M. Dent & Sons, 1908.

Mystical von Hügel, Friedrich, *The Mystical Element of Religion*, 2nd edn, vols 1 and 2. London: J. M. Dent & Sons, 1923.

Petrine Von Hügel, Friedrich, *Some Notes on the Petrine Claims*. London: Sheed & Ward, 1930.

Reality von Hügel, Friedrich, *The Reality of God and Religion and Agnosticism*, ed. Edmund Gardner. London: J. M. Dent & Sons, 1931.

Selected von Hügel, Friedrich, *Selected Letters, 1896–1924*, ed. Bernard Holland. London: J. M. Dent & Sons, 1928.

'Spiritual' von Hügel, Friedrich, 'The spiritual writings of Father Grou, S.J.' *The Tablet*, 75 (2589) (21 December 1889): 990–1; 75 (2590) (28 December 1889): 1029–31.

Insurrection Ward, Maisie, *Insurrection versus Resurrection*. London: Sheed & Ward, 1937.

'Evelyn' Watkin, E. I., 'Evelyn Underhill'. *The Month*, 22 (July 1959): 45–50.

Letters Williams, Charles (ed.), *The Letters of Evelyn Underhill*. London: Longmans, Green, 1943.

Evelyn Wrigley-Carr, Robyn (ed.), *Evelyn Underhill's Prayer Book*. London: SPCK, 2018.